/return this item by the last date shown.

...phone call is charged at local rate,
...umbers as set out below:

...m Area codes ...23 or 020:	From the rest of Herts:
...3 471373	01438 737373
...23 471333	01438 737333
...1923 471599	01438 737599

...ct.org/librarycatalogue

A Visit to New Zealand

BOOKS BY J. B. PRIESTLEY INCLUDE

FICTION

Adam in Moonshine
Benighted
The Good Companions
Angel Pavement
Faraway
Wonder Hero
Laburnum Grove
They Walk in the City
The Doomsday Men
Let the People Sing
Blackout in Gretley
Daylight on Saturday
Three Men in New Suits
Bright Day

Jenny Villiers
Festival at Farbridge
The Other Place : short stories
The Magicians
Low Notes on a High Level
Saturn Over the Water
The Thirty-First of June
The Shapes of Sleep
Sir Michael and Sir George
Lost Empires
It's an Old Country
Out of Town (The Image Men – I)
London End (The Image Men – II)
Snoggle

COLLECTED PLAYS

Volume I	Volume II	Volume III
Dangerous Corner	*Laburnum Grove*	*Cornelius*
Eden End	*Bees on the Boat Deck*	*People at Sea*
Time and the Conways	*When we are Married*	*They Came to a City*
I Have Been Here Before	*Good Night Children*	*Desert Highway*
Johnson over Jordan	*The Golden Fleece*	*An Inspector Calls*
Music at Night	*How are they at Home?*	*Home is Tomorrow*
The Linden Tree	*Ever Since Paradise*	*Summer Day's Dream*

ESSAYS AND AUTOBIOGRAPHY

Midnight on the Desert
Rain upon Godshill
Delight
All About Ourselves and other Essays
  (chosen by Eric Gillett)
Thoughts in the Wilderness

Margin Released
The Moments and other pieces
Essays of Five Decades
Over the Long High Wall
Outcries and Asides

CRITICISM AND MISCELLANEOUS

The English Comic Characters
English Journey
Journey Down a Rainbow
  (with Jacquetta Hawkes)
The Art of the Dramatist
Literature and Western Man

The World of J. B. Priestley
  (edited by Donald G. MacRae)
Trumpets over the Sea
The Prince of Pleasure and his Regency
The Edwardians
Victoria's Heyday
The English

A Visit to New Zealand

J. B. PRIESTLEY

HEINEMANN: LONDON

William Heinemann Ltd
15 Queen Street, Mayfair, London W1X 8BE

LONDON MELBOURNE TORONTO
JOHANNESBURG AUCKLAND

First published 1974
©J. B. Priestley 1974
SBN: 434 60360 0

Printed in Great Britain by
Westerham Press Ltd, Westerham, Kent

This book is dedicated to the friends –
whether only a few or a surprising
number – we made during this visit.

Contents

Illustrations

(The first ten pictures are by the author)

ix

between pages 140 and 141
Cowdie Forest on the Wairoa River, 1840, by Charles Heaphy
Meeting with Chief Hongi, November 1827, at Korarareka,
by Augustus Earle
Christchurch Town Hall: auditorium photographed by Robin Smith;
views of the exterior photographed by Martin Barriball

Notes on the Artists

Wong Sing Tai   Born at Otaki, N.Z., 1943; studied art and industrial design at Wellington; awarded first prize Benson & Hedges Art Award, 1968.

Nugent Welch (1881–1970) Born in Akaroa, N.Z.; studied art at Wellington; Official War Artist, 1918–19; member of the Council of N.Z. Academy of Fine Arts.

John Weeks (1888–1965) Born in Devon; studied in N.Z., at Edinburgh and in Italy.

R. J. Waghorn   Born Banks Peninsula, N.Z., 1898. Entirely self-taught, has exhibited in N.Z. since 1924. Member of Council of N.Z. Academy of Fine Arts and past president of Association of N.Z. Art Societies.

Douglas Badcock   Born in 1922; his work is represented in many public and private collections in New Zealand and overseas.

D. R. Neilson   Born in 1924; a prolific artist who has painted in Antarctica as a guest of the U.S. Government and has been represented in an exhibition in Paris arranged by Unesco.

Gaston de Vel   Born in Belgium in 1924 and studied in Brussels. After fifteen years spent travelling and exhibiting in Europe and Africa he came to live in N.Z. in 1961.

John M. Crump   Born in Wellington in 1943; abandoned schoolteaching in favour of full-time painting in 1970.

Peter McIntyre   Born in Dunedin, 1910; studied in N.Z. and at the Slade School, London; an Official N.Z. War Artist in World War II.

Preface

Not long after our return from New Zealand, last year, I contributed
to the *Observer Magazine* a brief and rather lively account of our visit.
To my surprise I received some letters, all from strangers, sternly
rebuking me for not offering them a study of the Maoris or the New
Zealand health service or its political situation. I hope these corres-
pondents will not waste time even turning the pages of this book. It is
not a study of anything. Apart from the final chapter, in which I try to
think about New Zealand, this book is what it clearly announces
itself to be. It is a reasonably honest and fairly intimate account of a
visit, where we went, and what I thought and what I felt during this
journey so far from home. If any readers think there is too much
about me in these chapters, I must remind them that I was the man I
was with all the time, that it is my experience I am trying to describe.
Some people can write as if they were really computers, but I am not
in that branch of my trade.

Along the way here I have in many instances tried to indicate my
indebtedness and offer my thanks. So, to take the chief example, it
ought to be quite clear how much I owe to the combined enthusiasm
and patience of Mr Derek Morris. But something more must be said.
I am very grateful indeed for the considerate help of the Ministry of
Foreign Affairs in Wellington and of Air New Zealand. I am indebted
too to Mr Melvin Day of the National Art Gallery, to the proprietors
of the McGregor Wright Gallery, to Mrs Janet Paul of the Turnbull

Library, and to Mr Maurice Dowthwaite, head of Heinemann's office in Auckland, all of whom, in one way or another, enabled me to reproduce the New Zealand paintings here.

The pictures reproduced here were chosen to give some idea of New Zealand landscape seen through the eyes of some of its painters, mostly contemporary. And I thank the artists concerned for permission to reproduce their work. Their strength only shows up my weakness, partly due to the fact that I was looking at the landscape through English eyes, peering through a haze that wasn't there. But unlike the other pictures, these modest *gouaches* of mine do illustrate my text.

Finally, at the London end of this venture, from first to last I have been greatly indebted to Mr Charles Pick, Chairman and Managing Director of Wm Heinemann Ltd, who, having visited New Zealand himself, was always enthusiastically in favour of a book recording my visit there.

J.B.P.

CHAPTER 1

Why and how we went

But why New Zealand? – they all said. And we had weeks and weeks of this. It was very odd. Certainly New Zealand is a long way off, but then for years we had been going great distances, from Death Valley, California, to the volcanoes of Southern Chile, Tashkent and Samarkand to Alice Springs in the Australian Desert, Tikal in the Guatemalan jungle to Hongkong, Canton, Bangkok, Angkor Vat in Cambodia. All this, and much more, had apparently been taken for granted, not a *Why* in sight. But New Zealand? – *New Zealand! Why?* As if we must be going out of our minds!

Certainly I didn't decide we ought to go simply to surprise my wife, Jacquetta, though it is equally certain that I did surprise her. We had returned some months before from a visit to Poland, where I had been – and enjoyed myself – as long ago as 1928. This time I came back, huffing and puffing, feeling exhausted. This was not the fault of the Poles, who had done their best for us. (Though the last place we had stayed in, a writers' hostel in decay and without writers, and suggesting a set for some unknown sad play by Chekhov, deflated our spirits.) But there is something exhausting about communist countries (even if the Poles are there), as if the Marxist-Leninist system never planned to have enough oxygen. Anyhow I felt exhausted and growled at Jacquetta: 'No more travel for me. From now on, no further than Tiddington!' – our nearest village. Yet the very next time I mentioned travel at all, I said, 'What about going to New

Zealand?' God knows I have my faults, but I can't believe even now that I am one of those *dull husbands*. Vain, egocentric, irritable, grumpy, tetchy, no doubt; but not one of those husbands whose wives know exactly what they are going to say next, fellows who would find it impossible to leap from Tiddington to New Zealand.

Going now into the *Why*, I must first announce that I wasn't invited to visit New Zealand. It was entirely my own idea. But when I called at New Zealand House in Haymarket, to ask some questions, I was received most cordially and even had a drink with the temporary High Commissioner, a most agreeable and civilized Mr Norrish. I said I wanted to visit their country because I had never been there, after going to so many places, and that I felt some sympathy with New Zealand because I disliked the Common Market and deeply resented being herded into it. (I keep being told I am a European when I know very well that I, like my father, my grandfather and my ancestors, am nothing of the sort. But do I want to be an eccentric 'off-shore islander'? Yes.) But while these reasons I gave were true enough, they didn't tell the whole story, going down to various levels, and it shall be told now. Odd though it may seem to people who don't write for a living, I have been a writer so long that I think it is easier for me to be genuinely confidential in print than it is in conversation. Incidentally, while I was in New Zealand – in Dunedin, to be exact – I was interviewed by a young woman employed by a serious periodical, and she wanted something longer and better than the usual perfunctory press chat. She confessed as soon as she arrived that after working out a list of questions, as serious interviewers do, she discovered that I had already answered them in one book or another.

Now for my story on the next level. It was December when I first called at New Zealand House. But in the previous August I had fallen victim to a complaint that was at first extremely painful and even later was damnably uncomfortable and inconvenient. So early in November I had an operation to prevent any recurrence. I soon discharged myself out of hospital – I don't like hospitals – but I didn't recover quickly, Nature at my age taking no further interest in me. Being the kind of bragging male bully who can suddenly look innocent, helpless, appealing, I was fussed over and implored to take it easy. But then I saw myself declining into a fat-lazy-fireside old codger, demanding and unproductive, a 200-lb parasite. To snap out of this, I needed a challenge. So what about going 13,000 miles – with Jacquetta of course – to pay a first visit to New Zealand? There was a risk of cracking up or at least feeling seedy more than half the time; but it seemed to me a risk worth taking. I *did* feel seedy at least half the time but I avoided doctors and treatments and tonics, and nobody knew except my wife. But she enjoyed the huge daft expedition, as I knew she would, and so, apart from the queasiest moments, for which my health and not New Zealand was responsible, so did I.

That is not the end of the *Why*; there is still another level. When I told one of my publishers I wanted to write a book about a visit to New Zealand, he dismissed the idea at once. New Zealanders didn't read books, and readers elsewhere cared nothing about New Zealand. Before I set out I was in touch with an editor I knew, who declared firmly that he would welcome any contribution from me – *so long as it wasn't about New Zealand*. In short, I was asked to believe I was bothering my head about a remote little country that simply wasn't important. And you might say that I flew 26,000 miles on a hunch that this was all wrong. It really was at that time just a hunch. But then I am – and always have been – a hunch man. I have been described before now as a very shrewd fellow, given to assembling and weighing up the pros and cons and the odds, whereas in truth I am not that kind of man at all. I am essentially an intuitive both in my life and my work. I never think carefully, never calculate, never bring together evidence. My mind jumps from one flash of intuition to another, hunch to hunch. And now I had this hunch that I ought to visit New Zealand, at whatever cost of time, energy and money, because instead of being unimportant it might, at this moment in history, be very important indeed.

Even so, I saw this as a book about a visit to the country. I wasn't competent to write a book about New Zealand, which would have to be based on six years there and not six weeks. But a book about my visit would be a different matter. After all, I would be with myself the whole of the time, and so could try to recall where I went and what I thought and felt. Such an account would therefore have to be very personal, quite intimate in fact; it couldn't be written honestly any other way. Readers wanting a treatise on the development of the country's agriculture and industry, a history of its early settlement and the relations between the Maori and the white immigrants, would have to look elsewhere. Even though I might end by offering some general conclusions – from which at this late date I can't be weaned – the chief question, perhaps the only question, I could answer truthfully would be this: How did this place and these people strike an old writer on his first acquaintance with them?

But now I am beginning, actually on the move. And because New Zealand is so far away, a brief account of how we got there doesn't seem to me out of place. We started with a pleasant daytime flight to Boston, there to spend two nights. This wasn't only to break a long journey but also to see friends who all live near Boston and are dear to us. (They are younger than we are but not young enough to live in an alien world that suggests a Somali village with electronic equipment.) In the morning after the second night, an American airline, which exists more sumptuously in its advertisements than in its actual flights, fastened us into its Jumbo jet, piped treacly music at us, and then shot us across the whole width of America to Los Angeles. We saw nothing, experienced nothing except tedium and false chummy speechifying. I remembered with regret the many train journeys I had enjoyed on the old Santa Fé route, where one morning, while still in bed, I would pull aside the curtain and see at last the South-Western desert again, vast and calm in the early sunlight. Now here we were, catching up with progress in this monster plane, a marvel outside and a bore inside, sacrificing the variety and flavour of travel to save time. I told myself that these days we were always either saving time or wondering how the devil (an interested party) to pass it and get rid of it. But then I was already feeling out of sorts: not quite ill but certainly not well and hearty.

At the Los Angeles airport we were met by the N.Z. vice-consul for Southern California, Mr Graeme Eskrigge, who did everything for us without appearing to do anything for us. He was both considerate and effortlessly efficient while at the same time illuminating all the proceedings with a gleam of irony, as if he knew – and he knew that we knew – that this fuss was part of a game we were playing. I took to him at once. Very foolishly making a mistake we did not repeat on our way home, we had decided not to spend a night or two in or near Los Angeles to break the long journey. But we had some hours to pass before the departure of our Air New Zealand plane. Much has been written about the evil sorcery of the time element in long jet flights. You have mornings that go on and on and still refuse to arrive at afternoons. You have evenings that seem to you to be artificial lunchtimes. There are midnights that are really 3.15 p.m. either yesterday or tomorrow. (On the flight to Auckland we mislaid a whole Wednesday.) Now add to this sinister confusion, which I was compelled to do, some sort of virus infection, however slight, and you have phantasmagoria.

This is why no figures will ever convince me that Los Angeles hasn't the largest and emptiest airport in the world. I seem to remember immense corridors, leading to nowhere in particular and with nobody else in sight, as if we had trudged into an unknown dimension. The whole fidgety business of air transport had apparently been suspended. Or we were lost in some uneasy dream; and soon there might be enigmatic figures standing and staring in those long corridors. Or we might now be travelling in some after-life. And indeed when I accepted a large whisky in the Air New Zealand lounge, it tasted as we are told such things will taste in the after-life – of nothing. (My fault, not the whisky's.) All it did was to augment the griping pains inside and the general phantasmagorical effect, still there as we set out on our long flight.

I have a sensible reason for disliking – and sometimes even dreading – night flights. Never had I been able to sleep, not a wink. On too many planes I have still been awake when everybody else – and I throw in passengers, cabin staff, and, for all I knew, even the chaps in the cockpit – had happily lost consciousness. (So I remember with affection the old Stratocruisers, which had a little bar down below where I could smoke my pipe and not pretend to be asleep.) The leaden hours would lumber by, and there I would be, dismally brooding away or looking at my watch, though it would probably be telling some nonsense time. Now, bound for Auckland, I faced a very long night flight, together with griping, nausea, and no possible help from food and drink, which Air New Zealand was prepared to supply in generous quantities. And only one break, at Honolulu.

However, it might have been worse. Indeed, it would have been a lot worse if the two cabin staffs (changing at Honolulu) had not been so extraordinarily attentive and kind. Instead of being a nuisance of a passenger, refusing this, waving away that, gloomily sipping milk, I might have been a stricken brother. They found some tablets, which had a dark antibiotic look, and after I had taken several of these I was gradually released from the griping and the nausea. I was able to stare at the strips of dawn light, and as these expanded and brightened I was no longer telling myself that after accepting a challenge I had fallen down before its first obstacle. With the sunshine a good conceit of myself, never long absent, began to return. Even so I was tired, weary down to my bones, so that I made a tottery descent of the steps going down to the tarmac of Auckland's airport.

At the foot of the steps, to greet us, was a broad-shouldered enthusiastic chap about forty, who introduced himself as Derek Morris from the Ministry of Foreign Affairs in Wellington. I was pleased to observe that he was quite unlike anybody I have ever met from our own Foreign Office, which banished enthusiasm about the time Lord Palmerston left it. As Derek Morris played an important part in our visit, I feel I must say something about him here and now. No doubt he had been saddled with us because, though a New Zealand civil servant, he was born and brought up in England, spending the first half of his life there. Without being a humbug, he had an English manner with us, a mixed style with academics and the like, and a very hearty first-names-at-once Kiwi manner with taxi-drivers and similar types – 'How's it going, Joe?' – though this may have owed something to his previous long spell as N.Z. vice-consul in Los Angeles. It was he who was responsible for our itinerary and made all necessary arrangements, keeping us company and driving us himself at the outset of our visit and then spending the final week of it with us. Even when he wasn't with us we almost felt he was – telephone messages, telegrams, letters streaming from him – and this was fine because we soon thought of him as a friend, from who we parted at the end of our six weeks most regretfully. Full of gusto and uncommonly energetic, he could include among his accomplishments a mastery of the telephone, which I have been using for sixty-odd years and always reluctantly and with distaste. But he always approached that instrument not dutifully but eagerly and almost with glee, picking it up as Heifetz might a Strad. Long-distance calls from roadside telephone booths – my idea of a chore in hell – were to him a joyous pastime. However, this strange enthusiasm was a great help to us, and indeed from first to last Derek was a rare prize out of the lucky bag.

We are now crossing the tarmac with him, a new acquaintance, and having some imagination he knew that the last thing I wanted was the TV interview, all rigged up in the airport lounge. (There had been many press announcements of our impending visit.) As I groaned, Derek told me I could keep the interview short and that it would be better all round if I got it over with. So I tottered nearer the TV lights and soon began croaking into the mike. Now the interview, brief though it was, contained one 'loaded question' – that is, a question intended to trap the interviewee into making a damaging admission – but somehow I floated above it. And the point here is this: *I never faced another 'loaded question' in all the TV, radio and press interviews I gave in New Zealand.* Every one of them seemed to be straightforward, honest, friendly. No wonder I began to like this country.

CHAPTER 2

At Waitomo

The hotel we had been booked into was more or less in the centre of Auckland. Within an hour we had taken a sharp dislike to it, and not unreasonably. It was one of those city hotels, not uncommon now, that are either still putting themselves up or already pulling themselves down. There was *hammer – hammer – hammer* all round us; we might have moved into a giant blacksmith's. Derek Morris had made a mistake – one of the very few he did make – and when he visited us that evening he freely admitted he had. There was some vague talk of leaving Auckland next day, changing our whole itinerary. I don't say his actual talk was vague, but it seemed vague when it reached us, full of bacon and eggs, always the safest order when all is dubious, and yawns and weariness. Undressed and stretched out at last, for the first time since Boston, 10,000 miles away, the Priestleys sank into blessed oblivion.

Next morning, newly-born as a brisk business-like fellow, I sought and found a bank, to change some dollars I had left over into New Zealand money. I was waited upon by a young woman with a square face and a determined manner that shattered my new and fragile persona of a brisk business-like fellow. Staggered by the news that my dollars were worth only 73 N.Z. cents, I found it increasingly difficult to communicate with the determined young woman. 'You know,' I said with a smile, for I was now assuming the role of an elderly English gentleman, 'you don't seem to understand what I'm saying,

8

though I speak quite plainly. Yet I understand you. Now why is that?'
She gave me a hard look: 'I speak louder,' and off she marched. Now
when I come to describe New Zealand's four cities I may be discovered approaching Auckland, the last of the four, not entirely
without prejudice. Could this be the *hammer-hammer-hammer* hotel –
or the young woman in the bank? But surely I can't be so easily
influenced, so childish? Or can I?

This turned out to be one of those mornings, rare with me, that
behave like expanding suitcases of experience: you wonder afterwards
how you packed so much into the time. I remember buying not one
Student Note Book but two. (I filled only four pages of the first one,
then gave up, wildly trusting a memory already in part-retirement.)
I remember being driven out, for it wasn't close at hand, to the New
Zealand office of my publishers, Heinemann. There I was given the
date, some weeks ahead, and the place, Wairakei in the middle of
North Island, of a Booksellers' Conference; and I agreed to pay it a
visit and speak a piece of some sort. And this, I knew already, would
change our whole itinerary. Fortunately, Derek Morris, in true civil
service fashion, had organized a little *Itinerary Meeting*, calling in
Professor Beadle and another expert. (Yes, the same morning, now
expanding incredibly.) The five of us, Jacquetta, Derek and I and the
two experts, sat around a table loaded with maps, looking as if we were
about to set whole armies in motion to carve up an empire. Overdoing
it of course, achieving that depth of gravity, that theatrical portentous
manner, which we almost always bring to events that we secretly feel
have escaped decent proportion, are playing out of their own league.
But an itinerary we could cope with did emerge. Just to prove how far
we stretched this morning, I will add that we had a hefty late lunch at
a much better hotel *at the far side of the city*. But when we sat down out
there, New Zealanders would have been saying *Good afternoon* for the
past two hours, for with them *afternoon* is strictly after noon, any
minute after midday, whereas with most of us English the morning
lasts until we have finished lunch. Many of our publishers, theatre
managers, assorted agents, must have the longest mornings in the
world.

Rather sleepy now in the warm afternoon, we set out by car to Waitomo, a four-hour stop for package tourists visiting its famous caves. But the Itinerary Conference experts didn't want to push us into caves. They strongly advised Waitomo because once its daytime flocks of tourists had come and gone it was a quiet place and had a good hotel. There, as Derek added, we could *relax* (more about this term later) and rest for a few days, well away from interviewers and all the media. And for once both expertise and the civil service were quite right. The pair of us still half-dotty after all that flying, we needed Waitomo.

The main road going south took us to Hamilton, where we broke our journey, two-thirds of the way to Waitomo. I noticed very little on the smooth fast ride between Auckland and Hamilton, partly because I still felt sleepy, but also because I seemed to be in England and not at the other end of the world. The only notable difference was provided by the large stands of fruit, all kinds apparently, at frequent intervals along the road. One after another was like an old Flemish still-life on a huge scale. The country behind those roadside stands, themselves so many harvest festivals, must have been bursting with fruit. We might have been travelling at fifty miles an hour along the edge of Eden. No, this was not another England, certainly not the England I had ever known, probably not even some long-lost England. Later I was to discover that while there are mountainous regions in New Zealand where little or nothing can be grown, in the fertile places most plants, even importations of all sorts, come shooting up, determined to be of giant size in the least possible time. Not being weary of men and their antics, there must be a lot of soil in these islands that is still innocent and eager.

Adding industry to agricultural marketing, Hamilton has mushroomed to a population of about 75,000, ranks under N.Z. rules as a city, and now has a university and this, that and the other. Between the factories and warehouses on the outskirts and a few substantial buildings in the centre, it gave me the impression, repeated many times later, of being a cleaned-up, nicely-painted shanty town, doing very well at present but ready if necessary to be pulled down and carted off elsewhere. A shop there, open for ten years doing the same trade, could be a famous old establishment. Parked near the central post office, so that Derek could do some happy telephoning, we went our several ways. After a moment or two, my dear wife, who probably includes a witch among her ancestors, simply vanished, a trick she can perform at all times and in all places, being, so to speak, her own illusionist. Needing some butane fuel for my lighter, I searched both sides of a shopping street for a tobacconist's. There wasn't a sign of one. It was then I learnt that although New Zealanders smoke, they have no tobacconists. You must buy your cigarettes, pipes, tobacco at a hairdresser's, which seemed to me about as sensible as buying shirts at an ironmonger's.

However, I returned to the car with some butane fuel. Derek was there, smiling, obviously refreshed by his telephoning, and then Jacquetta suddenly appeared – doing her vanishing act in reverse – bearing a modest supply of booze. When travelling we buy some booze for our bedroom, not because we are a pair of alcoholics, grabbing the whisky or gin bottle as soon as we wake up, but because we like a stiffish drink, usually the first of the day, just when we have come out of a pre-dinner bath and have dried but have not yet dressed ourselves. This pleasant conjugal habit-cum-ceremony saves money too, especially in New Zealand, where the tots of spirits in the bars are the smallest in the world. Even a 'double' is barely visible, and you begin to feel you are taking part in some dangerous chemical experiment with minute samples of poison.

We were just about to get into the car when a youngish man, hot, breathless, eager, came rushing up. He introduced himself as the director of the local museum. Jacquetta Hawkes mustn't leave Hamilton without visiting his museum. Derek and I went along with them, though I doubt if I would have gone if I hadn't agreed to write this book. It was an odd sketchy sort of place, with narrow wooden stairs going up to a fair-sized room that looked as if it had only just stopped – reluctantly too – being a warehouse. It was housing temporarily a show of East Indian designs. In a sort of cubby-hole office the director, glowing with pride and joy, showed us the treasures he had lately acquired. These were several old Maori combs, black and battered and with some of their teeth missing. I am not sneering at his enthusiasm – I like enthusiasm – if I add that I couldn't share his pride and joy and must have turned a lack-lustre eye on these objects. While the others discussed the combs, I was asking myself a question, one that I carried with me during the next few weeks, allowing it at times to guide my impressions, before attempting a reply to it.

What happened was this. While the Maori combs were being so proudly displayed, I remembered that Jung had suggested somewhere that the soul of a conquered people enters, and tends to dominate, the unconscious of their conquerors. (There are plenty of examples that support this idea, but to discuss them would take us too far away from the question I asked myself in Hamilton.) Now would I find that among younger and perhaps more sensitive and imaginative New Zealanders, no longer aware of the British background, perhaps deliberately rejecting the British heritage to affirm their New Zealand nationality, the Maoris would seem more and more important, their traditions and history and way of life, their legends and arts, filling and then enriching a vacancy, a new blankness intolerable to the upper levels of the unconscious and consciousness alike? And here I was not resting my case – or the original question that began to shape it – on Jung's more profound or complicated idea of the invasion of the soul of the conquered. For all I know the Maori soul may stay at home and never go wandering. But I had a hunch – and after all it was another hunch that had brought me to this country – that I had here a question that would be worth answering when I knew more.

During the fifty miles or so between Hamilton and Waitomo there was a change of landscape. It was not a dramatic change. The mountains to be seen in so many New Zealand travel advertisements were not arriving. But rather rounded limestone hills made their appearance. They were not bare like those I knew so well in Yorkshire. They offered plenty of foliage, sometimes in dark clumps halfway up and often clothing the tops; but I had no idea what trees, what bushes were there, not only being ignorant but also having to stare out of a

A sketch of the late-afternoon scene from the viewpoint high above Waitomo,
North Island. I presented it to Mr Kirk, the Prime Minister,
who had asked for one of my sketches

Distant view of Wellington, North Island. Only included because
my eldest daughter, herself a painter, liked it

View along the road not far from the Dalgety
homestead, South Island

Early morning impression of one of Mount Cook's
smaller companions, South Island

car window in a fading light. However, when we were close to
Waitomo there was light enough to discover that it was set against a
background of fairly high hills, promising country for *gouache*
sketches. The place had been well chosen for a few days' rest, beyond
the reach of the media. As for the hotel itself, it was larger and more
imposing that I had imagined it would be. And indeed it received us
most hospitably and provided us with ample accommodation. (This
last is an important point. On more than one occasion later we had to
cram ourselves and our luggage, packed for a six-week visit, into
rooms designed for one-night guests with attaché cases. And the
newer the hotel or motel, the smaller, the more maddening and
claustrophobic their bedrooms, with space we badly needed taken up
by TV sets we didn't want.) Hotels like private houses have their own
atmosphere, and the one at Waitomo, which perhaps remained our
favourite, had an unusually *easy* atmosphere that pleased me, not a
man who loves hotels.

Oddly enough, this was one of the hotels owned and run by the
Tourist Hotel Corporation, a state enterprise and therefore not
usually associated with easy atmospheres. But perhaps the temporary
manager at Waitomo, Don Pollock, was working the magic. Whenever
I ran into him, he greeted me with a broad smile and said, 'Everything
under control?' This was friendly but absurd because I had nothing
to control, not even my temper, everything being so pleasant, whereas
he had a large hotel and its staff to control. Or if he didn't do it
himself, he had been clever enough to find somebody who did.
Running this place would have been a nightmare to me. Coaches filled
with package tourists on their way to the caves would arrive during
the late morning – sometimes, I believe, at rather short notice – and
there could be a couple of hundred of them, knowing they had already
paid for a substantial lunch and were now ready for it. (Many of them
had that anxious look I have noticed before among 'carefree' package
tourists.) And it was not long before Don Pollock's staff, with
everything under control, were ready for them.

What follows may be common form in large tourist hotels all over
the place now, but this Waitomo routine was the only one I have lived

with for several days, so I propose to describe it. The side of the big dining-room that faced the windows had a counter running almost the whole length of it. Behind this counter were two or three chefs – or at least men dressed like chefs. On the counter was an astonishing variety of cold meat – everything, you might say, except buffalo hump or roast swan – and further along was a dizzy choice of vegetables and salads. A long line of tourists moved steadily forward, took plates, pointed to what they wanted, were served by the chefs and then removed their loaded plates to one of the tables, where waitresses brought them any drinks they wanted. All was orderly – no jostling, no fuss – and smoothly efficient. And the food, which usually included a hot dish, perhaps curry, together with various icecreams and fruit salads, was excellent. When it is spread out for the eye like this, some people become astoundingly greedy; I noticed several middle-aged female tourists returning *a second time* from the counter with plates still thickly loaded, and no doubt falling asleep later in the caves.

Watching this daily show of efficiency made me wonder if the easy New Zealand manner, the hearty shirt-sleeves-and-shorts style, didn't mask quite a talent for organization. They look and sound, these chaps, as if they could hardly bother to keep the country running, but then you find they are running it very well. And how could so few people have done so much? Unless of course – and it is an uncomfortable thought for an Englishman – too few people are less of a handicap than too many people.

There might have been a few New Zealanders among the tourists on this lunch conveyor-belt but the majority of them were either Americans (a surprising number of these) or Australians. Some of the waitresses were also Australians. It seems that many New Zealand and Australian girls share a dislike for waiting at table *in their own country*, so they cross the Tasman Sea to hide their blushes. Kate in the bar, handsome enough but rather more severe in appearance and manner than most barmaids, didn't suggest either side of the Tasman Sea, and finally she told me she came from Birmingham and intended soon to return there. She'd had a fancy, she added, to see something of

the world. I have heard this more often from young women like Kate
than I have from young men, that is, if we ignore the hippy types who
wander, half-dazed and nearly broke, anywhere between Piccadilly
Circus and Nepal. Unlike them, the Kates have everything under
control, at least on the surface, where we encounter them, safely and
well above the ecstasies and tears of feminine private life.

Our transport and local expeditions had now been left to Mr Pasco
and his taxi service. Mr Pasco did not resemble any of the later drivers
we had; he suggested a Victorian actor-manager renowned for noble
parts; but he was like the rest of them in two respects – he was
pleasant and obliging, and like them he gave us without stint a mass of
information about the locality, never personal, political, aesthetic,
but always topographical, geographic, commercial, as if an estate
agent was performing a duet with a civil engineer. It was Mr Pasco
who insisted that I should visit the unique Kiwi House (Jacquetta,
mistakenly assuming that this would mean a long drive, had chosen to
go for a walk. Actually the place was only a few miles away.) The Kiwi
House may have been unique, but it was no tourist attraction; Mr
Pasco and I and the man in charge had it to ourselves. At first I could
see nothing alive within the netted enclosure, which was artificially
darkened to persuade the Kiwi couple that it was night and time to
poke around and feed. Staring hard, I saw they were darkish brown,
about the size of a fat, short-necked goose. They have very long beaks,
with nostrils at the far end, to smell out grubs; and whiskers at the
near end, the creatures not only being nocturnal but also short-
sighted. I was told they lay extra-large eggs and that it is the male,
rather smaller than the female, which has to incubate them for about
75 days – altogether a triumph for Women's Lib in birdland.

I could well understand that such a creature, found only in New
Zealand, might fascinate a zoologist; but after ten minutes or so,
straining my eyesight to watch this pair slowly rooting around, I must
confess that I had had quite enough of them. What I couldn't understand was why this wingless night-grubber had ever been chosen as
New Zealand's national image. It was a bad move. New Zealanders
should never have called themselves *Kiwis*. Perhaps it has been the

Kiwi aspect of New Zealand life and character that encouraged visitors in the past to call them dull. Though not a unique native of the country, the glorious albatross would have been my first choice.

The weather remained fine and warm, and we passed our mornings, without Mr Pasco, climbing a little hill behind the hotel, finding a place where I could sit and paint and Jacquetta could set out for an exploratory walk. I have three of the sketches I did then on my desk now. One of them, concentrating on a pyramidal clump of dark trees crowding a hillock, is just passable. The other two, vertical scenes (unusual for me), are sad failures. Both look up the hill, again towards dark foliage, but one begins from a group of over-size weeping willows, obviously successful immigrants; the other starts with a ghost tree, its branches dead-white; and both hillsides, in my sketches, try to show fantastic outcroppings of blackish limestone without any success at all.

My fourth and better paint, which was to have an odd future (it was given to the Prime Minister to hang in his office), I owe to Mr Pasco, who, late one afternoon, suggested that on his way to pick up some children from a remote school, high above the hotel and village, he should leave me at a Viewpoint. New Zealand, I discovered later, is devoted to these Scenic Viewpoints, paving them and providing them with seats. Our drivers shared this devotion and so rushed us to the nearest Viewpoint, believing disastrously that a man who was trying to paint would prefer to cope with some vast panorama, and would be happy to do so with other Viewpointers looking over his shoulder. However, here above Waitomo I was alone, and seemed to be no longer on a hill but up a mountain. I felt that something might be done with the enormous prospect that was just beginning to gather dusk. Two real mountains, far away and tiny, were still golden and hopeful in sunlight, symbolic peaks, and it was with an eye, equally hopeful, on them that I began my sketch.

However, our most rewarding afternoon came when Mr Pasco took us to the neighbouring town of Te Kuiti, there to call by appointment on Mrs Rangimarie Hetet, famous for her skill in the almost lost art of creating the traditional feathered cloaks, once proudly worn by the

most important and warlike of the old Maori chiefs. She received us –
and I use the term deliberately – in the small front sitting-room of her
bungalow. Only half-Maori herself, for her father was an English
surveyor, she had grown up with her mother's people and had
married a Maori. Calm, quiet, upright in spite of her 80 years, Mrs
Hetet was my idea – and it is one I rarely entertain – of a great lady.
She had called in, probably to do the talking, her married daughter,
Mrs Te Kanawa, who lived a few miles away: quite a different type,
more the extraverted Maori, amiably voluble, eager to instruct and to
demonstrate. It was she who brought in the various cloaks of feathers
that her mother had designed and toiled over, probably for months at
a time. One was bright with parrot feathers; another – not traditional
this, the old Maoris never having known the bird – resplendent with
pheasant feathers; yet a third, not the most gorgeous but apparently
once the most important, plucked from the Kiwi. I was delighted to
see these feather-cloaks but on such short acquaintance did not quite
know what to think about them; they belonged, so to speak, to a
debatable area between the strangely barbaric, the handsome, and the
genuinely beautiful. But there could be no question of the queenly
Mrs Hetet's talent for design displayed over and above the cloaks
(probably destined for museums) in tapestry weaving and splendid
capacious bags.

Now that we come to the actual yarn, the basis of all these creations,
spinning being traditionally a feminine mystery, I shall pass any
description over to Jacquetta. 'The material used for all purposes is
the so-called New Zealand Flax,' she begins in her notes, 'a plant with
very long (3 to 9 feet) spear-like leaves belonging to the agave family.
The Maori name is *Harakeke*. (From the time of Captain Cook it was
much sought after for such things as mending rigging, etc, and
became quite a considerable export.) It grows wild in damp places all
over the country.' Returning to our afternoon, she continues: 'The
correct Maori way of preparing the flax was demonstrated for us by
Mrs Te Kanawa. With a mussel shell held in the palm of her hand she
stripped off all the green underpart of the flax, leaving behind the
tough, straight white fibres. For good weaving this should be washed

and scraped again, but our samples that were immediately spun have remained white and soft. The spinning was done by rolling the fibres on the outside of the thigh. It was done with extraordinary speed and it was impossible to see the different methods used for the three samples. The finest of these has about 12 fibres and is used for weaving. The thickest, with a double twist and spun much tighter, is mainly used for the tassel-like appendages sometimes seen on the feather cloaks. In the skirts, now so much used for dancing, etc, and called *Piupiu*, lengths of flax are alternately scraped and left intact, then steeped in a special dark mud. This blacks the exposed fibres while the unscraped sections curl up into pale-coloured tubes. The total effect is to have stripes of dark and light – patterns being obtained by grading . . .'

As I write this, after having thanked Jacquetta, here on my desk are the three samples of yarn produced by mussel-shell-leaf-stripping, done quite quickly, and then by that lightning and almost magical lower-outside-thigh sleight of hand. And here they are, these short lengths of yarn, unchanged, strong as ever, ready to outlast me by innumerable years. I think my pleasure in them and in the way they were made, so simply and swiftly, partly derives from the fact that my youth was spent in Bradford, an industrial textile centre, where spinning mills of blackened stone went roaring away, pouring smoke out of their tall chimneys. I don't say they could be replaced by mussel shells, spearlike leaves, clever hands and dutiful thighs: that would be asking too much. But there ought to be some kind of compromise between Mrs Hetet's front room and those huge roaring black mills.

Then Mrs Hetet, saying nothing, and her daughter, telling us everything, took us along to the Te Kuiti meeting or 'carved' house, a Maori creation but not old, dating from the late nineteenth century. It was about the size of a smallish nonconformist chapel but with a startlingly different interior, being ringed round with big-headed, small-bodied carved figures. At first glance they looked like so many rather sinister idols but were in fact figures representing ancestors. If Mrs Kanawa, who was busy explaining everything, explained why a fair number of these ancestors were putting out their impressive tongues, then I can't have been paying attention. There was nothing challenging and derisive about these tongues, which might have been put out at the request of a doctor; but of course there must be more in it than that. Later, in museums, I saw older and more impressive Maori carving, and perhaps if I had lived with it, instead of just staring and walking on (probably wishing I could smoke), the impression I had of it might have changed. As it was – and perhaps still under the influence of my first encounter with it in the Te Kuiti meeting house – while I found it skilful and often most ingeniously designed, its general effect was unpleasing, too grim, revealing none of the more gracious, smiling, carefree aspects of Polynesian life. Coming upon those ancestors was like blundering, at a bad moment, into a meeting of a grotesque war cabinet. But not for any money would I have taken aside the magnificent Mrs Hetet and told her so.

After our fifth and last night at Waitomo, Mr Pasco arrived to take us to the Tongariro National Park, where we would stay three nights at the Chateau – a large hotel, not anybody's castle. As visitors to Waitomo we must have been unique, not only because of our comparatively lengthy stay, so many of its tourists not staying more than half a day, but also because we kept away from its famous caves. This is not strictly true of us as a pair; Jacquetta did visit one of them, the one with all the glow-worms shining in it, very prettily too, she reported. But I never went near any of them. As far as I was concerned, Waitomo might have been caveless. The truth is, I don't want caves. One of the things that happened to me in the First War was that I was buried alive, in a trench below Vimy Ridge, by a *Minnenwerfer* exploding at the entrance to a small dugout where I was busy dividing up the platoon rations that had just come up the line. I don't say that this left me a victim of claustrophobia. After all, to write a piece about miners during the Second War, I crawled along, like a giant worm, to the very coal face. But this was something, I felt, that had to be done; if miners were doing it every day then at least I could do it once. (And, after all, that was 30 years ago.) I saw no point, however, in going underground again just to say I had seen some caves that I didn't want to see. What both of us wanted from Waitomo was what it gave us – some easy quiet days, together with an hotel we much enjoyed, before we began travelling again, to stare and to admire or to scorn, to make notes, to meet people, to give interviews on TV and radio. Jacquetta, fully rested, was now ready for the long solitary walks she loves. Though still a bit queasy inside, I was a better man than the one who landed at Auckland and I was eager to produce some satisfying *gouaches*. Good on you, Waitomo!

CHAPTER 3

Tongariro and its Chateau

Along the road between Waitomo and Tongariro National Park, on a warm bright morning, very soon the landscape began to assert itself. Scenery sprang up all round us. I wasn't tempted to stop the car and take out my paints: though it was beginning to be impressive, I didn't feel it was my kind of scenery. But the picnic lunch we ate – a farewell hospitable gesture from the Waitomo hotel – was my kind of lunch. Jacquetta was even happier than I was, just because we had parked in a little rest place that was on the edge of the *bush* – that is, the original virgin forest of gigantic trees with an undergrowth of tall ferns. It had covered most of this and other regions, but the earlier settlers had set fire to it to clear the ground or later, wanting timber, had taken saw and axe to it. What the timber trade left behind was so much melancholy scrub, which, like all those growths that nobody wants, insisted upon spreading and spreading. Jacquetta had now enthusiastically adopted the bush, which appealed to her both as a collection of unfamiliar flora and as an idea, a symbol of ravaged and defeated nature. Though Mr Pasco told us that the timber industry was almost finished, as we moved on towards the National Park we did see, to Jacquetta's disgust, a few men still felling some bush. So she declared that not another acre of this extraordinary antedeluvian forest should be allowed to go, neither here nor anywhere else, at least in North Island. I was ready now to bet money that on any future long walk she would make straight for any remaining section of the bush, being the victim of a vegetable love affair.

21

Mr Pasco announced that he proposed to take us on a detour that would bring us to a remarkable Viewpoint. I was not in favour of this diversion, chiefly because almost always I dislike turning aside when I am on my way by car to a particular destination – in this instance, The Chateau. However, I said nothing, and it wasn't long before I was glad I had made no objection. The Viewpoint was a wonder. It was high above Lake Taupo. (*Largest lake in New Zealand; area of 250 square miles; between 300 and 400 feet deep; first seen by any European in 1836.* During the last week of our visit we were to stay on the opposite shore, at the very edge of the lake.) That day, at least at the Viewpoint, the lake was calm, still, and seemed to cover everything with a delicate blue haze. Most of its surface might have been burnished pewter. The white massed clouds above the far shore were reflected in vaguer vertical strips. Not a sound reached us. This was a lake out of another and better world. Romantic beauty had arrived at last. Painting was not to be thought of up there, with other View-pointers around and no good place for my gear, so I did a hasty pencil sketch, hoping, quite idiotically, to recapture the magic later when I brought out my colours. But of course I couldn't. Only a Turner could have discovered in his memory and then transferred to paper all that light and stillness and enchantment of blue air. A Priestley would have needed several lifetimes, toiling with pencil and brush every day from dawn to dusk, hopefully to attempt the scene. Even so I had my magical moment, a 'peak experience', at the Viewpoint, though I suspect now that it was responsible, as we shall see, for my finding Tongariro National Park itself disappointing as a painting prospect.

After leaving the Viewpoint we climbed our way into the Park. (*163,356 acres; includes three volcanoes – Mount Ruapehu, 9,175 feet, the highest in the North Island and active at times; Ngauruhoe, 7,515 feet, constantly active; and Tongariro, 6,517, mildly active. Mount Ruapehu is the ski-ing playground of the North Island. These regions are surrounded by native forests, open grassland, and subalpine vegetation.*) An odd thing – but once we were inside the Park, for a brief period we might have been in Scotland. Apparently, not so long ago, in the 1930's I believe, a Mr Cochrane decided to plant some heather in the lowlands here, and it spread like purple wildfire. We might have been on a Scottish moor; even the distant volcanoes played a temporary part in the act, looking not unlike Highland peaks. The road approaching The Chateau was a poor thing – we were told it was soon to be widened – but the actual forecourt, up a ramp and then displaying dignified lamps, was most imposing, as if royalty or a conference of prime ministers might be on its way there. Imposing and very large as it appeared to be, there seemed to us no sensible reason why this particular hotel should be known as The Chateau. It was obviously a 1920's imitation-Georgian job, and our bedroom – quite big, thank Heaven! – showed us a lot of pseudo-antique furniture. (The hotel, always indicated on every map of North Island, had been built by private enterprise in the 1920's, but after some disappointing years had been taken over by the state's Tourist Hotel Corporation. We never took to it as we had done to the Waitomo Hotel. It was large and pretentious and yet at the same time seemed under-staffed, so rather flustered by the arrival of coachloads of tourists, mainly American. No sooner had we unpacked than Jacquetta went off for her first walk, returning exalted to report 'a most superb, golden and fiery sunset, with the mountains and imitation moors all burnished'.

After dinner, not a memorable meal, we took our coffee in the huge lounge with Mr Mazey, the chief Park Warden or Ranger, who was paying us a visit from his headquarters not far away. A pleasant intelligent man, he came ostensibly to offer Jacquetta some advice about possible walks within the Park, but very soon the talk broadened out, over a drink or two, into general conversation. He had attended, most happily too, a conference of National Parks wardens and rangers in America – to be exact, Colorado. This claimed my attention because in the 1930's when I had explored and written about the American South-West, I had been enthusiastic about the National Parks and their ranger services, and had exchanged some friendly letters with the head department in Washington. After I had told Mr Mazey that I hoped the American National Parks were as good now as they were nearly 40 years ago, he made a point with some emphasis, though amiably enough. During his stay in Colorado, he had never come across any of the things reported to be darkening the American scene – no riots, no savage vandalism, no muggings, and so forth.

After accepting this, without suggesting that no conference of hefty Park rangers could be expected to run into trouble, I asked him what the attitude of the Mazey family was towards Britain. He replied that his parents had always regarded and spoken of Britain as 'home', that he himself had drifted away from this attitude without definitely adopting any other, and that his children simply saw Britain as just another distant place. I had similar replies later from other people I questioned, though several of them admitted that while Britain might be 'just another distant place' to the young, many of them could not resist the huge magnet of London. Incidentally, I was already discovering, rather to my dismay as an Englishman far from home, a woeful lack of British 'hard news', as distinct from flimsy magazine material (publicity about TV performers and the like), in the New Zealand newspapers.

We were collected firmly next morning by Mr Mills, who was to be our Tongariro driver. Though equally amiable and determinedly informative, he was quite different in appearance and character from Mr Pasco, being thick-set and powerful, curly-haired and ebullient, fundamentally good-natured but apt to play an aggressive role in the stories he told, as if defying invisible enemies. He had a passion, not shared by the Priestleys, for hydro-electric schemes, though perhaps it was only one that we kept drawing nearer to, whatever the chosen route. On this beautiful morning, Mr Mills and I dropped Jacquetta to begin her walk and then went tootling around looking for something I wanted to paint. It was difficult to decide on anything. There might be some exciting stuff high up near the volcanic craters, but here down below what could be easily seen appeared to me dull, utterly charmless. As Jacquetta's walk was far more rewarding, I quote her hasty but revealing notes on it. 'I climbed up to a mountain lake a few miles away. I mounted through fine bush with huge *rimu* (red pine), three varieties of tree fern – silver, black and soft – this last the commonest with "skirts" of hanging dead fronds. The black, with very dark main stems, is by far the most beautiful. The lake, in a small crater, is completely surrounded by bush. The water quiet; the great archaic trees coming down to its edge, and with a few dead blackened trunks, lying in the water like reptiles, giving a sense of the primeval world. The bell birds and a *tui* sing and call. It might be an age before Man. I don't think I have ever felt so completely, so beautifully, by myself.'

Descending to the road, Jacquetta was duly picked up by Mr Mills, and I stopped my painting (not good) to join them. We lunched on a promontory – not far from a hydro-electric works – where a late (1830) Maori trading station had been excavated. Jacquetta, the professional, thought nothing of the excavations – two huts and a potato pit, with one hut dubiously restored, roofed with corrugated iron, fenced with hideous barbed wire – no, no, not good enough! But, all the same, a fine place for a picnic, warm in the sun and with a regatta of white clouds in the cerulean sky. During the afternoon I made a more determined effort to do a decent paint. I have it in front of me now – and it still won't work. It shows me a foreground of long grass and scrub; a narrow and mysterious sheet of water ending in the left middle-distance in some sort of canal; on the far side of the water a long and very bright bar of something like sand; and further to the left a purply-brown mountainous mass, not badly indicated; and high above all, and best of all, diaphanous trailing clouds in the blue. Where I ran into trouble was with the water and that very bright sandbar or whatever it was. First they were too hard and then, trying to correct this, I got them too smudgy. The truth is, quite apart from any deficiency in technique, I was still being defeated by New Zealand light, only superficially like ours and really, in painting values, quite different.

I had had to leave the road and settle down among long grass to do this sketch. To my surprise, within a minute or two Mr Mills had also settled down there, not more than a yard away from my left elbow. Clearly he longed to be helpful, to act as a sort of painter's mate. I was sorry I couldn't give him the painting equivalent of those orders that surgeons rap out in their operating theatres: *The Yellow Ochre again! More Zinc White! Naples Yellow – sharp! Now the big square brush!*

Olive Green, come along! But it couldn't be worked, not on this first occasion, and, unknown to us, there was not going to be another one. Undoubtedly there is something about painting that not only fascinates, demands to be watched but is also powerfully infectious. One later driver, after watching me for hours during our first day, turned up two mornings afterwards with some strange efforts of his own. These might have been preferred by some trendy art-gallery director, welcoming them as Naïve Primitives, to my tediously conventional efforts, belonging at best to the *avant garde* of 1873.

The next day, a Friday, may be said to have been blotted out of the calendar: the only day of this sort we suffered during the whole of our stay. Not only did it rain but the Park, even the nearest road, vanished. Anybody or anything moving ten yards away from the door of the Chateau would have disappeared; but in fact nobody seemed to arrive or to leave. It was as if the Deluge had been announced. All day we were marooned. I don't know what other people felt, but for my part I react less violently against such a complete blank of a day than I do against teasing weather, the kind that lures you out and then rains hard when you cannot find shelter and then, when at last you are sheltered, slyly lets you see the sun again. In the utter blankness of a day like this Friday, I settle down, without feeling frustrated and indignant, to do nothing in particular – read a little, write a letter or two, potter and poke about. It was all rather like being in a motionless liner without the sinister foghorn.

At one end of the big lounge some noisy middle-aged men – and why are some middle-aged men so noisy? – played carpet bowls. Just beyond them a young couple monopolized the billiard table, perhaps to improve their game, which was very sketchy. But could this and the bowls have been happening all day? Possibly not, but they seemed to be. The bar, deep down in the basement, ought to have been crowded and uproarious, but it wasn't when I went down there. It was empty and sad, as if the ghost of a bar was haunting the basement. Meals were a welcome break, but they would have been even more welcome to us if their main courses had been served in a different fashion. They came – as they did in too many other places until we stoutly objected – piled up on one large oval plate – meat, vegetables, garnishings (and the inevitable tomato), the lot, such a brutal hotch-potch that it repelled appetite. We never found this monstrous custom in private houses. Why had hotels adopted it? Did it come out of some lingering pioneer tradition or was it recent, an attempt to please American tourists with eyes greedier than their bellies – as we used to say in the Army? This blank Friday might have been a good day to settle this question (I never did settle it), but reading, writing, poking about and pottering and yawning, I was in no mood for serious research. So the hours crawled into night.

On Saturday we had to go to Wellington, awaiting us with a heavy programme. Mr Mills was still in charge of us. The National Park looked as if it had just come back from the cleaners. All was very clear, very bright, with the volcanoes black cut-outs against the deepening blue of the sky. A few patches of snow had come from somewhere. The scene in every direction looked far more paintable than before, but that of course was because I was leaving it – the ironical department working hard as usual. The country we passed through was at first very steep, suggesting many hillsides that had been de-forested, looking vaguely wrong like newly-shorn sheep. Then we descended into meadow land, and began to see more sheep at pasture than we had ever seen before: they didn't look quite real. I think Mr Mills took us to a Bulls 'teashop' for a snack lunch (not bad) in order to repeat a joke of his youth – *Wellington gets its milk from Bulls.* I used the quotation marks above simply because New Zealand seems to describe all its roadside cafés, eating-houses, places of refreshment, as either 'teashops' or 'tearooms', which suggests to us something quite different, lady-like establishments delicately run by the daughters of late Indian Army colonels.

Mr Mills, older than he appeared to be, gave us an account of his family: one son in Australia combining industrial management with writing a book on gardening; another son, presumably the youngest of the family, still at school nursing an ambition to be a teacher of engineering; and daughters who were all nurses. But how many daughters? Again, I can't remember; I doubt if I ever knew. The truth is – and here and now the reader is warned – I am one of the worst men in the world to remember anything accurately during a longish car journey. (And there were to be a number of these during our visit.) While I can't fall asleep in a moving car, I can't keep wakeful and alert. I wander into an unrewarding middle ground between the two; I am in a stupor, like a man who has taken too small a dose of some narcotic or, the night before, took too large a dose. This does not shorten the journey but tends to lengthen it. Time and space, possibly as a rebuke for my lack of attention to what they have to offer, enlarge themselves. However, I was wide awake when Mr Mills, going round and round the centre of Wellington, vacant and empty because it was Saturday, tried to find our hotel, so new that it hadn't existed when he was last in the city. But at last we did find it – and with it Derek Morris, planted firmly near the reception desk, waiting to go through our Wellington programme with us. And it needed some going through; there were to be no yawning layabout days in Wellington. After all, this city is the seat of government, which might be keeping its eye on us.

Distant view of Queenstown, South Island

Landscape near Queenstown, South Island

Late afternoon on a road near Queenstown, South Island

Coast scene near Dunedin, South Island

CHAPTER 4

At Wellington

We made a bad start in that new hotel. Like many new creations it was clever-silly, offering us boastfully things we didn't want and refusing us things we did want – space, for example. We dined in the hotel restaurant, which was making a half-hearted pretence not to be in Wellington, New Zealand, but in some more exotic place. It was staffed by two or three solemn young men, who looked as if an inspector from Michelin might arrive at any moment; and by haughty statuesque blondes, fine girls no doubt but certainly not natives of that exotic place. The dish we ordered as our main course had been prepared by a reliable chef, but then had been ruined by all that piling-up-one-plate custom I have already denounced. Having had a long day, we went to bed fairly early, but were not allowed to sleep. Outside the hotel but within hearing distance there was a *discothèque*, which boomed and blasted away and never stopped until 2 a.m. – Sunday morning too! My wife's brief note tells all: 'Cannot understand this savagery,' she wrote.

A clear warm Sunday, bringing out all the cars. Now in charge of transport with his own home town, Derek took us out sightseeing, with the possible chance of a paint somewhere. But first a Viewpoint, at the top of Mount Victoria, with a lot of other people around, many in family parties. And certainly the view of Wellington from up there is magnificent. This is a city that lends itself generously to Viewpointing. Its distant clusters of little houses, brightly painted, ravished the eye and kindled the imagination. Oh – to be a Wellingtonian and to live, without going to an office, in one of those little houses! True, after a week in the city, my final impression was very different. Being the seat of government, Wellington has some imposing buildings, but even so, as a local man (not Derek) pointed out, it also has an untidy unfinished look, as if nobody quite knew what to do with it. Then it is very hilly, and as I was kept busy there all day and half the night my chief recollection is of riding in cars that did U-turns and then went roaring dizzily up steep and narrow sidestreets, secretly terrifying me. Nevertheless, I carried away with me that first Pisgah-sight of it from Mount Victoria.

Our next stop was far below, at Makara Beach. As this was a fine Sunday, there were of course too many people who had gone there in too many cars. But I must add that not since childhood and early youth have I been a beach man. I am a heath man, a moor man, a downs-and-hills man, but not for me this popping in and out of the sea, lolling on the sand, grilling yourself as if you were a steak. I am not bigoted about this; I have friends I still admire and treasure who will travel thousands of miles to do their beach-work. But from some dark corner of my mind there comes a whisper that there is an element of vanity here, that girls and women with good figures love to get out of their clothes, and that even some members of my own sterner and nobler sex have what we might call 'a magnificent-torso complex'. Most people at Makara seemed to have brought picnic lunches, but there was a little tearoom not far away, to which Derek went striding purposefully, returning in triumph, almost as if he had found gold, to report that fresh crayfish and salad were ours for the asking. Inspired perhaps by the crayfish, we merely moved round the corner to discover a tiny bay or inlet that had no beach but also had no people. Apart from some black-backed gulls flashing around, we had the place to ourselves.

It had a solitary white cottage set against some darkish foliage, and I see now, with the sketch in front of me, that I painted those trees very badly. One hillside behind it was covered with gorse in bloom; the opposite hills were bare but not sharp and bright; and just off centre, against the aquamarine horizon was one of those very dark clumps of trees that New Zealand obligingly provides painters with, to use as an accent. Not far from the cottage, jutting out into the foreground water, was a tiny promontory where the gulls rested between their flashings. The scene was almost like another glimpse of my favourite painting country, the West of Ireland, yet somehow lacked – and I can't tell how and why – that country's curious magic. (No doubt myth and legend come into it, and any Maori substitute doesn't work for me, a stranger. New Zealand has a surprising number of good poets, but it needs a great poet, like Yeats.) And now for the melancholy conclusion. I finished my sketch with some satisfaction; Derek, on the spot, liked it; Jacquetta, returning from her walk, praised it; but now, staring at it on my desk, it seems to me a poor thing. The thousands of miles between Wellington and Alveston, Warwickshire, have robbed it of all juice and flavour. Perhaps it serves me right for secretly considering Derek's crayfish rather boring.

We attended that night an agreeable dinner party given by Mr and Mrs Turnovsky. A successful business man, Mr Turnovsky was said to be deeply concerned with the arts and was certainly very much a Unesco man. Here I must explain that I was involved with Unesco in its earliest years, being a U.K. delegate at its first two conferences, then saying goodbye to it because I thought it was being organized on the wrong lines. Jacquetta, a principal then in the Ministry of Education, was even more involved because Unesco affairs in Britain were her responsibility. Moreover – and what is really more important – we first met through Unesco; to my mind its greatest triumph. And now, at the Turnovsky dinner-table, here was our old acquaintance, the great Kiwi Unesco man, member of its Executive Board, Dr Clarence Edward Beeby, C.M.G. We stared at him in amazement. It was quarter of a century since we had last seen him and he didn't seem to have changed at all, not a hair, not a wrinkle. The H-bomb had been developed; there had been wars in Korea and Vietnam; the girls had shortened their skirts, the young men had grown their hair; the Permissive Society had arrived, together with droves of illegitimate children; men had walked on the moon: yet here was Dr Beeby looking and sounding exactly the same. How had he done it? Why can't we all do it? I don't think Jacquetta asked him those questions as they talked after dinner. I suspect they were deep in old *Unesco* gossip, capable of offering some highly-flavoured depths.

My man after dinner, when his lively wife, a gynaecologist, had been hastily summoned back to work, was Mr Bruce Mason. He reminded me that we had met in London in 1944, when I urged him, if he wanted to write, to go back to New Zealand and his roots. He is not only a writer now but also must have considerable skill and power as an actor. He has given many hundreds of successful one-man performances, not only all over New Zealand but as far away as the Edinburgh Festival, of what he calls *A voyage into a New Zealand childhood*, aptly entitled, after Thomas Wolfe, *The End of the Golden Weather*. He sent me a copy of this piece, and I found it a nourishing mixture of close observation, humour and poetic feeling. In his Introduction, Mr Mason gives a spirited account, too long to reproduce here, of how he encountered a sullen, abusive farmer ('I'm damned if I'm coming to see high-falutin crap!') who secretly attended his performance, returning shaken, moved, enthusiastic, really a changed man. Politicians and others who object to public money being used to subsidize the performing arts should read that Introduction by Mr Mason. On my part I was glad to know that he had flourished, after following my advice so many years ago.

I spent Monday morning looking at pictures. This was pleasant enough but there was business in it too, for I was anxious to choose some typical New Zealand landscape paintings to be reproduced in this book. First, I went to the National Art Gallery, where the director, Mr Melvin Day, was very helpful indeed, then and afterwards. As I have dealt with my choice of pictures in my Preface, I need say no more about it here. However, being told that a one-man show had just opened at the McGregor Wright Gallery, I went along there. Not a large gallery, rather cramped, but I was surprised to see how many pictures had already been sold, presumably that very morning. The painter, Mr John Crump, was quite a young man, clearly delighted by his success but modest enough in talk. Taken into a back room, to be shown work by other artists, I spotted three landscapes that might suit my purpose, though, like the two by Mr Crump, I couldn't guarantee they would appear in this book. But altogether a satisfactory morning.

Being full of painting I decided in the afternoon to have a go myself, with Wellington my subject. So Derek Morris ran me up to Khandallah, where, in a children's recreation area, with hardly any children around, I could settle down and paint what I could see of the city across the bay. I worked hard at the sketch but in the end it disappointed me; somehow it lacked colour and life, not capturing what I knew to be there in Wellington. Much to my surprise and a bewilderment that still lingers, when back home many weeks later I was showing my N.Z. *gouaches* to my eldest daughter, a better painter than I am, she was enthusiastic about this particular sketch – all the more surprising because she had been to Wellington too. So now, as I write this, before the final choice of illustrations has been made, I don't know whether this sketch should go in or be left out. But then readers of my age or thereabouts will understand me when I add that there is more and more I don't know – and not just about pictures – for the years thicken the mists of bewilderment and widen area after area of ignorance. God help us all! – there was a time when I felt I knew almost everything about anything worth knowing.

Fortunately, no examination had to be passed that Monday night at the Victoria University of Wellington. All was ease and good talk. We were dinner guests of the Vice-Chancellor, Dr Taylor, late of Peterhouse, Cambridge – and an Irish charmer. (Actually he's an Ulsterman, but he stays here as an Irish charmer.) Mrs Taylor, smiling and twinkling away, represented the Kiwi charm department. Jacquetta and I felt a stab of remorse at the very outset of dinner. For our hostess had procured some rare oysters, and we had to tell her that neither of us liked oysters. But certainly all was ease and good talk after that. Jacquetta was happy discussing Jungian themes with Professor Roberts and his wife. What I discussed, in post-prandial mood, I cannot now remember. I do recall a striking-looking and far from ancient bibliographer, said to have an international reputation; but I am sure I didn't talk bibliography with him for though I have lived with books for well over 50 years I have little interest in that subject. (There must be at least 10,000 books in this house of mine, but never have I collected first editions, special editions, signed copies, rare issues; I just acquire books.) But I do remember contrasting very sharply this evening with one I had spent, some years ago, with members of the staff of an Australian university, fellows who seemed to have gone sour because they felt so remote; whereas Dr Taylor and his colleagues were so cheerful, open, friendly, not worried at all because they were such a long way from Oxford and Cambridge, London or Manchester. The difference in general atmosphere had had its effect even among the dons of the two countries.

Tuesday found us in or near the grandiose Parliament Buildings (though the House of Representatives looks like a cosy City Council chamber brought up to date with microphones); we entered and departed through mysterious little side-doors; and between entering and departing we moved, as boldly as we knew how, along the 'corridors of power'. Yes indeed, Tuesday was our seat-of-government day. Our first appointment was with Mr Corner, head of the Ministry of Foreign Affairs, who had spent some time representing his country at the United Nations, where in fact New Zealand has commanded more attention than any other of the smaller states. He had a courteous manner and a sharp decisive mind. When I said, rather tactlessly, that I thought the U.N. had now committed itself to the membership of far too many tiny new states, he declared, though not aggressively, that these had often shown very good sense and that the real weakness of the U.N. was largely the fault of the great powers. He spoke incisively of other matters that need not concern us here. Finally, he described with genuine warmth – no senior civil service humbug – his mounting admiration for Prime Minister Kirk, whom we were about to meet, discovering in him unusual mental ability in general as well as political astuteness. He had found in Mr Kirk a man of ideas who pondered deeply and was ready to consider any new idea brought to him. And I thought to myself that if there were many successful politicians ready to ponder deeply and consider new ideas, I hadn't had the luck to meet them.

So Mr Corner took us along to the P.M.'s room and left us there. The man behind the desk was a big man, with huge shoulders and a large strong face. It was an open face with something still boyish about it, in spite of his 50 years and hard experience, which began during the Depression when he went out to work at 12. Like a few other men I have admired and taken to at once, he was entirely self-educated, but that self had been a good master. He greeted us warmly, without any sign of that conscious importance which so many successful politicians can't resist, and gave each of us a book inscribed with his good wishes – a rare out-of-print work on volcanoes for Jacquetta, a handsome art book for me. As soon as we began talking I understood at once what Mr Corner, describing him, had meant. He spoke slowly, almost gropingly, very much a pondering man, without any flashy answers. I knew that he saw New Zealand now not as the remotest member of the British Commonwealth but as a modest but self-determined South Pacific power; and so I suggested more help for the arts in their capacity to shape and colour and establish a national identity. To which he replied he was hoping to increase an annual subsidy for recreation and the arts. And I think – and if I am not quite sure, it is because the subject turned up more than once around this time – I put forward certain ways in which New Zealand writers, with so limited a home readership, could be helped apart from subsidies.

After some further talk on these topics, Jacquetta made a conservationist plea, hoping there would be no more destruction of the primeval bush, to which he replied, in a more political style now, that while he agreed in principle this preservation would have to be balanced with keeping up employment, with housing, and so forth. (Jacquetta said afterwards that if she had felt like arguing with a P.M. she would have told him that after a generation or so of this balance-maintaining, the bush would have entirely vanished.) One regret I had afterwards, remembering this talk. I didn't know then, as I was soon to learn, how some sensitive souls among the electorate were disgusted and often appalled by the callous (not deliberately cruel but thoughtless) treatment of so many of New Zealand's wretched beasts, doomed to undergo unnecessary suffering, all of it sadly out of key with the country's humane record. A law or two could end it, and, had I known, I would have appealed to Mr Kirk's large humanity and sense of compassion, about which I have no doubt whatever. Indeed, I say again, I took at once to this big pondering man.

We lunched with Mr William Sheat, Chairman of the Queen Elizabeth II Arts Council. Among his other guests were Mr Nikolaidis, salaried director of the Council, an enthusiastic lady responsible for the Downstage Theatre, and Mr Ian Cross, a novelist of considerable talent who made a fine start with his *The God Boy* but was now, I gathered, working in public relations. I felt rather a fraud accepting Mr Sheat's pressing invitation. I had never served on our own Arts Council in any capacity, and for my own theatrical enterprises I had never asked for nor received a penny of public money. However, I could make a few personal points. One weakness of this N.Z. Arts Council at that time was that it badly needed but could not afford at least six salaried representatives, one for each of the four main cities, then one for Northland and another for the extreme South. These were jobs for professionals, however modestly paid; amateurs, no matter how enthusiastic they might be, couldn't really cope.

We discussed, as I had to do later that day and possibly had already done during our talk with the P.M., how N.Z. writers could be helped quite apart from larger government subsidies – by fellowships from outside sources, by introducing more of them into the universities and so following the American example, and of course by establishing lending rights. I made a final point about contemporary arts in general that particularly applied to New Zealand, though I knew they had created problems elsewhere. There was far too wide a gap now between the big public and the small but eager *avant garde*. This gap could be closed by what we could call large-scale *primary* artists – not to be dismissed as too highbrow, too lowbrow, too experimental, too conventional – but the sad truth was that we were desperately short of such primary artists. And so on and so forth. I was astonished to learn afterwards that this lunch had been described as an exhilarating occasion, because, with due respect to Mr Sheat and his hospitality, it had seemed to me not quite depressing but, shall we say, pitched in too low a key.

Back to officialdom in the afternoon, keeping an appointment with Mr P. O'Dea, Secretary for Internal Affairs, in which capacity he would be responsible for administering any fund for the arts. I found him a sympathetic but cautious man, not as Irish as his name. Much of our long talk returned to cover ground I have already described. He did say, however, that he felt that the public should not have to pay for what none of them wanted – clearly having in mind extreme *avant garde* work. I seem to remember pointing out, matching his amiability, I trust, that all my adult life I had been helping to pay for things I didn't want, from bowling greens to bombing planes. I asked him too to remember that in the face, heavy with disapproval, of an unsympathetic public, young people concerned with the arts tended to overdo *avant garde* fashions, gleefully adopting shock tactics. (Later I was to see evidence of this in one or two of the public art galleries – work that was trendy to the point of sheer silliness.) However, I liked Mr O'Dea, and when office hours were over and Jacquetta looked in from one of her museums and there was no harm in taking a drink, all was pleasing sociability.

The evening took us out of seat-of-government Wellington, for we had accepted an invitation to dine with the Manson family, whose son, a handsome quiet young man, was due to conduct a TV or radio interview with me. His parents, our host and hostess, had lived, I believe, a longish time in England before settling here. But Mrs Manson was a New Zealander while her husband was English, very English, like a heartier and more artistic Galsworthy Forsyte, with witnesses to his concern for the visual arts round all the walls. They gave us an excellent dinner and what turned out to be, in Jacquetta's words later, 'a cheerful family party'. The last arrival, late in the evening, was a Maori poet who said very little, something few poets can do late in the evening. We were driven round the bay, back to our hotel, by my prospective interviewer, and so came, well content, to the end of a very full day. It was even fuller, I believe, than I have reported, one or two brief visits of mine and various archaeological and anthropological doings of Jacquetta's having been omitted. But then enough is enough!

Wednesday kept us even busier than Tuesday did; it also offered us an extraordinary variety of commitments and events. The morning was devoted to what might be called, though not in terms I favour, 'exposure on the media'. It began with an unnecessary press conference, probably the result of the civil servant in Derek Morris fighting his way out to insist on something. Hardly anybody bothered to turn up at 10 a.m. in our hotel, and I couldn't blame the absentees, for after all there had already been a lot of publicity about our visit and we had been asked to do TV and radio interviews. I have not wasted money and time subscribing to press cuttings for the last 40 years or so, but somebody sent me afterwards a piece describing that 10 a.m. confrontation, and it begins as follows:

> He came in slowly and hesitantly, a bit like a sleepy old bulldog early disturbed. He was dressed informally; baggy grey slacks, black carpet slippers, badly stained unpressed jacket, stringy tie . . .

Only the first three words are strictly accurate: I did come in. The rest is on the wild side. I was only dressed informally if a black cutaway morning coat, grey striped trousers, a stiff high collar and a silk cravat had been expected; and after all this was neither a wedding nor a funeral. The slacks I was wearing were not baggy but are in fact rather too tight. My slippers were neither black nor carpet. Certainly my jacket was unpressed, but then Wellington was leaving me barely time to shave, let alone sending clothes to be pressed. I think this reporter must have been sitting some distance away from me. The only person sitting very close was an extremely pretty girl, who never said a word but gazed and gazed at me, perhaps memorizing those stains on my jacket. However, she cannot have thought I looked like a bulldog or she would have sat further away, well out of biting range. The broadcasting session that follows need not be described, but it does persuade me to make one general point. I did a fair amount of TV and radio on this visit. Previously I had done some broadcasting in seven or eight different countries. But there was less huffing and puffing and fussing in New Zealand studios than I had found anywhere else. Whatever else the New Zealander may be, he is no fusspot. This helped to confirm what had occurred to me at Waitomo, that behind the country's easy and casual manner and style there is an uncommon ability to organize things both efficiently and coolly.

Derek had set up a lunch at a restaurant, crowded, very popular, called the Woolshed. (Wellington restaurants like to pretend to be something else, as if a suggestion of a masque appeals to the city.) We were there to meet Denis Glover, poet, publisher, typographer. Possibly because he was busy elsewhere, fortifying himself for the occasion, he was so late we began lunch without him. Finally he arrived, with a silent friend, rather like the straight man in a comedy duo who had forgotten his lines. Denis Glover's persona, covering the poet who winced in his verse, was that of a rumbustious stentorian character, and at first I felt he worked too hard at it. But soon I liked him. 'I tell you,' he roared at me, 'I want to go and tell the English people what I think about them.' To which I replied, without asperity, 'And I tell *you* – the English people wouldn't care a damn what you thought about them.' And I liked him even more for the bellow of laughter this brought from him. Risking unseemly interruption – though in fact he was quietly attentive – I invited him to attend the lecture I was giving that night at the University. Later, I greatly enjoyed his collected poems in *Enter without Knocking*, which he kindly sent us. And as this book of mine is aimed at British and American readership and not simply at New Zealanders who know his work, I will quote a very short poem as a tasting sample of his economy and understatement and his very personal blending of the sardonic and the sad. It is called *Solitary Drinker*:

> *Standing in the same old place*
> *He thought 'I know that silly face,'*
> *And there beneath the spirits shelf*
> *The mirror showed his silly self.*

He saw himself with some surprise
A sorry sod with headlamp eyes
AFORE YE GO *the slogan read,*
But he stayed on and stared ahead.

'I cannot stand this blasted place,
I cannot stand my blasted face.'
The public bar was through the hall :
It had no mirrors on the wall.

There are other moods of course: this is a good poet. But then there are some good poets in New Zealand.

Lunch over, I had to hurry along to the Alexander Turnbull Library. (Named after Alexander Horsburgh Turnbull, who bequeathed to the country his magnificent collection of books, manuscripts, maps, documents of the early settlement.) It was Jacquetta, who had already been there and delighted in the place, who urged me to see it, especially to look through the prints and water-colours of the early settlers. So I could not spend as much time as I wished with Mr Bagnall, the Librarian, and was very soon deep into the art department, under the combined spell of the old watercolours and prints and of the head of the department, Mrs Janet Paul, who might be described as a delicious example of blazing feminine enthusiasm. I needed just two pictures to be reproduced in this book, and it was hard to decide which two would be best when so much of this early work was captivating. But a choice was made, and then, on leaving, I was presented by the delectable Mrs Paul with two port-folios of prints: *Six Views by Sir William Fox* and *Five Early Views of The Hutt and Wairarapa by Captain William Mein Smith*; and now here they are at home with me in Warwickshire, a pleasant link with New Zealand, Wellington, and the splendid Alexander Turnbull Library.

Music came next. Unfortunately I was never able to attend a performance by the N.Z. Symphony Orchestra, but I caught the last ten minutes of that afternoon's rehearsal and they seemed to be giving a good account of themselves. Tea was being provided in a side-room, and here I renewed my agreeable acquaintance with Alec Lindsay, now the leader of the national orchestra. The last time we had met was when I had gone to Daytona Beach, Florida, to write a little book about the London Symphony's season there. (This had seemed to me so gloriously daft when I read about it, that I decided to be equally daft and – but no, I refer the curious to my book, *Trumpets Over the Sea*.) Alec was leader of the second violins in the L.S.O. but told me even then he would soon be returning home to join the N.Z. Symphony. There is in my book a spirited photograph of him and another player just back from fishing and looking as if they had had too much sun and beer. But now, on this afternoon, surrounded at the tea-tables by fellow players and other interested persons, he made a neat complimentary speech about me, because I cared about orchestras and had been of some help to their men during the war. I made a brief reply, not half so neat. And that, to my regret, was the last I saw of Alec and his orchestra, for as usual they were moving around and while I was too, our paths remained wide apart: 'Two stars,' as we were told long ago, 'keep not their motion in one sphere.' But I like to think there is symphonic music in New Zealand, all under the sharp eye and masterful bow of Alec Lindsay.

Jacquetta agreed with me that there was no point in her attending my lecture, which she had heard before, so to quote her notes: 'I was collected by nice Mrs Paul to dine in her half-restored cottage. One climbs up to it by a long, very steep and rough footpath that seems more country than town. Joined by her friend Nan, a historian. Much improvisation of domestic equipment and elderly feminine giggling.' Meanwhile, Vice-Chancellor Taylor had taken me on to a platform to face a large and apparently enthusiastic audience up at the University. His Chairman's introduction was deft, humorous, just the right length. I mention this because most chairmen's introductions are cumbersome, tedious, much too long. I had called my lecture *Duality in the Drama*, a new but better title for an old lecture, originally commissioned by the Old Vic, delivered afterwards in many different countries. It found its way into print, together with a number of appendices, as *The Art of the Dramatist*. The lecture was going splendidly when about two-thirds of the way through – and I was giving it entirely without notes – I suddenly felt I had had enough of it. I wasn't boring the audience but I was boring myself. So I cut it short, but after a longish vote of thanks, not by Dr Taylor, I whispered to him that perhaps so good an audience deserved a little more entertainment and I would tell a few theatrical stories. These went 'like a bomb' but as in some previous encounters with bombs, I found myself and the whole audience plunged into total darkness for two or three minutes; but I went on with the tale I was telling, being an old black-out hand, and this seemed to delight everybody.

After this performance, Dr and Mrs Taylor's 'reception' at their house immediately rose above the name they had given it, transforming itself into a crowded lively party, which is just what performers and performees need. (But all depends first on the hosts – and the Taylors had the knack of it.) Jacquetta had brought Mrs Janet Paul. New acquaintances began to look and sound like old friends; social gabble seemed witty or deeply significant; glasses were filled and refilled; in short, quite a party. On the way home I reflected, no doubt a trifle muzzily, on the wide scope of this Wellington day. Consider it! – all the media in the morning; a poet at lunch; early settlers and old watercolours, then music, in the afternoon; the nature of drama in the evening; and the night bringing a rollicking good party. And I remembered what I had been told when I had decided on paying this visit: 'A beautiful country but otherwise dull'; they had said, 'terribly dull people, old boy'.

After two full days when we would have preferred to take it easy, Derek was apologetic about his Thursday arrangements. Some people at Massey University, Palmerston North, had pressed him to send us there to attend a lunch, and after some initial resistance he agreed at least to ask us. We were against the trip; we knew nothing about Massey University and didn't want to spend several hours in a car; but feeling that we might let Derek down we accepted the invitation. It was a warm day; and though it is only about 90 miles from Wellington to Palmerston North, somehow in a hired-car with a driver we didn't know and without any scenic splendours on view, we found ourselves, grumbling inside, on a longish tedious journey. Through spic-and-span but monotonous streets of detached villas, we were driven straight to the house of Professor Batt, head of biochemistry at Massey, who was giving the lunch. After two minutes with him, I realized that this was really Jacquetta's party. Her father was Gowland Hopkins (incidentally, cousin of the poet), a legend among biochemists who was awarded a Nobel Prize for his work on vitamins; and Professor Batt worshipped his memory. This was all to the good. It was time the big guns sounded for Jacquetta, who, I must add, had not only kept so many Wellington engagements with me but had also busied herself with her own professional concerns, exploring the Historic Places Trust with Mr Kineky; the Alexander Turnbull Library, of course; the Dominion Museum with Dr Bell and his two ethnographers, Mrs McFadden and Mrs Mackay; and had had a good session with Mr Jock McEwan, Secretary for Maori and Island Affairs, leaving her as knowledgeable about all these matters as I was deplorably ignorant. High time indeed that academic New Zealand should honour Jacquetta with a party!

Moreover, to our surprise and delight, it was a good party. Professor Batt was a youngish lively man with an attractive wife. The leading members of faculties he had invited included no droning old bores. (Now I come to think of it, I was probably the only droning old bore there.) Food, drink, talk – all were excellent. I discussed wine with, I think, two members of the English Department; but I am not sure now if we had been long enough in the country to decide firmly, as we did later, which local wines we liked best: these were *Montana Pinotage* among the reds and *Cresta Doré* of the whites. I learnt something after lunch that nobody had mentioned before, namely, that applications for or enquiries about jobs came in a steady stream from American academics. If this pleased me, it was not because I felt malicious about American academics – not in the least. But when I had discussed the prospects of this book, ready to accept some guidance from a man in the book trade I know very well, he warned me that American publishers and readers would take no interest in such a book, caring nothing about New Zealand. But he himself had never visited the country. And from the first day in Waitomo I had found large groups of American tourists all over the place – and earlier there had been a fair number of American expatriates escaping from any nuclear Doomsday in the northern hemisphere – and now I heard about all these applications for academic posts.

Like the good lunch party it was, it went on longer than it ought to have done. The result was, gladly fulfilling a promise, we were shockingly late when we arrived at the Bertrams' house, not easy to find, somewhere on the far edge of the Lower Hutt Valley. We had met them earlier in Wellington and indeed once, some time ago, in England. Professor Bertram is a clever and widely-travelled man, on the staff of Wellington's Victoria University. Mrs Bertram is an almost ruthless enthusiast, more passionately concerned about flowers, shrubs, trees than I am about anything except the fate of the bedevilled human race. After apologies for lateness were offered and accepted, we took our glasses of sherry down into the back garden. There, to my surprise and Jacquetta's delight, probably not more than ten yards away was a green wall of dense vegetation – the original primeval New Zealand bush. What an astonishing thing to have in one's back garden! And to have a ravine full of it when one is commuting to Wellington and its University! Virgin forest and higher education all mixed up! Am I not right in proclaiming that this is an odd, original, uniquely attractive country, well worth anybody's visit?

As this has been a long chapter already, there must be some *huddling* now between Thursday evening and our flight to South Island on Saturday morning. Just for the record, then. We were to have dined at the house of Mr Corner, but his Foreign Affairs suddenly called him to Auckland. So his agreeable second-in-command, Mr Millar, together with the equally agreeable Mrs Millar, took us to Plimmer's Restaurant (the best yet) where our fellow guests were Sir Guy Powles (once governor of Samoa, now Ombudsman) and Lady Powles, and the founding father of the Ministry of Foreign Affairs, Mr Macintosh; and we all dined well and talked well. On Friday morning more TV; then we lunched, again at

Plimmer's, upstairs in a private room too, with Dr Conrad Bollinger from the English Department of the University, looking too dashing and romantic to be 'a fan' of mine, though wanting to do a piece about me: a pleasant occasion in spite of the intrusion of a photographer. What I did during the afternoon I can't recall, but probably I went the round of hairdressers trying to find some decent tobacco. As this was our last evening in Wellington we had invited Derek Morris and his splendid wife, Julia (English but like an unmartial and sensible Brünnhilde) to dine with us, the restaurant they chose being *The Coachman*; and there we went and 'fleeted the time carelessly as they did in the golden world'. We already had in our possession Derek's *Programme for South Island*, which had probably many happy hours at the telephone behind it; he took us to the airport on Saturday morning, put us into the plane for Christchurch (a smallish jet, new to me, comfortable and almost cosy), and waved us away to the South Island and all its mysteries. We were to return to the North Island before we went home, but not to Wellington, for which we now felt an affection; and certainly one of us would never see it again in this life. *Wellingtonians* – for the occasional jutting underlip, the scowl or poached-egg stare, the *basso profundo* interruption – I beg your forgiveness!

CHAPTER 5

At Mount Possession

Though we landed at its airport, we didn't go into Christchurch, Mr Steele driving us straight up to Mount Possession. But what is all this? Who was Mr Steele, why Mount Possession, and what were we up to? These are good questions, doing what they were intended to do, giving me an excuse to bring in an explanation. In London I ran into Mr Rupert Withers, Chairman of Dalgety, who knew we were about to visit New Zealand and kindly invited us to stay a few days at Mount Possession. This is a sheep station in the Canterbury High Country – and high it is, for there was a mountain well over 7,000 feet not so far away – that originally belonged to the Acland family but has been recently acquired by Dalgety. It runs to about 36,000 acres, has the largest flock of merino sheep in the country, about 22,000 ewes, together with about 2,000 head of cattle. It boasts a homestead over a century old (what bold builders they were, the old settlers!) that is now the residence of Mr Dobbs, the manager of the station, and his wife and three children. Mr Steele, who met us at the airport and drove us up there, was one of Dalgety's Christchurch managers. End of explanation.

Not really knowing where we were but already aware that this was the South Island and somehow quite different from the North Island, we climbed steadily, going through pastoral country, leaving townships behind and passing named hamlets that seemed to consist of a corner store and a garage. I began to feel a long way from anywhere in particular. A narrow and roughish side-road led to the homestead, which, in neat trim, gave no sign that it was over a hundred years old. It was a wide bungalow-type house that had two painted wooden gables and between them, covered by the roof and supported by white iron pillars, a verandah admirably adapted for lolling around. In front was a large lawn surrounded by borders bright with flowers. The house faced the way we had come, down the valley, and you had to go round the side of it to catch a glimpse, above the tall hedge, of the rising country that would keep on rising until it reached the majestic Southern Alps, well out of sight here. Later that very afternoon, with the light still clear, I was taken only a few miles further along the main road and did a paint sitting in the grass alongside it. My sketch shows a greyish-brownish foreground, so much grass suffering from the drought, an inexplicable dark-red plateau jutting into the middle distance, and behind it some rounded peaks of no great height but yet wearing some patches of snow. It was a good place for painting, but I never did it justice.

The house itself was rambling and had a few rather dark passages in it, so that it took me some time to find my way around and to stop opening wrong doors. It was chiefly those wrong doors, and neither a word nor a look, that made me feel I must be rather a nuisance round the place. Mr Dobbs himself, manager of the station, was away mustering, which meant that he and his men were bringing down all those thousands of sheep from the higher pastures, soon to be blasted by winter, to lower ground. I had seen pictures of mustering and so understood why I hadn't been invited to attend this performance of it. The job was bad enough without old guests trying to tag along. Mr Dobbs made a solitary appearance in the homestead, to take a bath and eat some decent food. He sat with us for a while, a tall, dark and rather gaunt man – or perhaps he looked gaunt after all that sheep-herding down steep hillsides. He had nothing to say and so didn't say it. Neither his silences nor his glances were unfriendly, but I don't think I am being too fanciful if I add that I detected in them a touch of irony, the irony of a man who has been working at full stretch and then finds himself in the company of people who don't seem to be doing anything very much. I wish he had mustered all that could be mustered, with the hard work all done, so that he and I could have sat at ease and had some good talk.

Mrs Dobbs, mother of three young daughters and the homestead's cook-housekeeper among other demanding roles, certainly wasn't one of those who weren't doing anything very much. She seemed to do everything, and do it very well. She had been a schoolteacher before she married Mr Dobbs, then a shepherd. In the earlier years of her marriage, I believe, she had lived in places so remote that they made the Mount Possession homestead seem like an urban social centre. Rather small and comely, with a bright searching glance, and tirelessly energetic, she combined high-speed housekeeping with obvious intelligence and a wide range of interests. We appeared to achieve mutual respect, not without a gleam of affection on my part, almost at first sight. Interviewed later, she flattered me: 'An extremely interesting and genial guest with a marvellous memory.' (I may be interesting; I don't know; but I am not particularly genial, and as I am discovering to my cost now, writing this book without notes, my memory is not marvellous but hardly adequate.) However, if I continue to set down Mrs Dobbs's qualities, this is not simply a matter of 'cutlet for cutlet'; it is because she occupies a unique position in this record.

She alone was the one New Zealand housewife I was able to observe at close quarters. This is easily understood. Elsewhere we lived in hotels, ate in restaurants or visited private houses only as guests for lunch or dinner, whereas we lived under the same roof with Mrs Dobbs. Nor is that all. Except on one or two grander occasions, we took our meals at one end of the large kitchen while Mrs Dobbs prepared them at the other end. Her food was excellent, coming fresh to the palate, a welcome change from the re-heated concoctions served all-piled-up in restaurants. What first astonished me and then continually fascinated me was not only the absence of all fuss and fluster, the economy of movement, the deftness of it all, but also the amazing speed with which she produced course after course. It was almost like conjuring. Why do Women's Lib propagandists refer to 'mere housewives' as if they were all so many blundering amateurish drudges? In my sight, Mrs Dobbs conjuring away in her kitchen was a brilliant professional. She deserved an honorary degree in house-wifery. She would have been better on TV than most of the pro-grammes I chanced to see in New Zealand. She ought – but wait; perhaps I am overdoing this. There may be thousands of N.Z. house-wives, many of them living in remote places ('Ten miles from a lemon,' as Sydney Smith said of his Yorkshire vicarage), who could match Mrs Dobbs's good-humour, sense and dexterity in the kitchen; but then I was never able to observe them – and now it is too late. But if such wives can be found almost everywhere, then a lot of Kiwi men have done all right for themselves, probably better than they deserve, if I know my grumbling wooden-headed sex.

On Sunday morning Mr Pat Goode in a big car came up from Christchurch to take charge of us. We saw more of him than we did of any other driver we had, and he certainly deserves a paragraph to himself. He was an excellent chauffeur, making speed when he could but always careful when he couldn't. He was also extremely patient, waiting for hours if necessary without a grumble or a sour look. But this hardly begins to describe him. He was at heart a *courier* not a mere driver. If the other drivers were full of information, he was even fuller. He was a guide-historian as well as a courier-driver. There cannot have been a stone-built house, barn, toolshed, on the road to Queenstown and afterwards to Dunedin, that he didn't point out, often giving us its history. (He seemed to us, to whom simple building in stone was no treat, quite irrationally proud of the stonework of the era 1850–70, as if he felt that there were giants in those days – as indeed perhaps there were: many of the earlier settlers were un-doubtedly remarkable men.) He was not without guile, as when he persuaded us that a visit to Mount Cook National Park ought to be undertaken because it was more or less on the way to Queenstown, our destination. (It was in fact miles out of the way.) But though he deceived us, it was from laudable motive, a patriotic guide-courier desire to bring us the majesty of Mount Cook. He was known and popular all along the route, so that any motel, tearoom or shop welcomed us. With all these people he was on easy terms, though never loud, never boisterous. With us he maintained a distance of calm courtesy, with just a suggestion, no more than a faint flavouring, of a gentleman's gentleman, the Jeeves touch. But we never had a better driver-courier-guide, and when he finally deposited us in Dunedin we were very sorry indeed that he was leaving us.

On this Sunday morning, a beautiful morning too, Mr Goode took us to the neighbouring station of Mount Peel, to lunch and spend the day with its owner, Sir John Acland. He is a member of a famous family; he had sat in the House of Representatives for some years; he had been Chairman of the New Zealand Wool Board, Vice-Chairman of the International Wool Secretariat; in short, a man well acquainted with public life and its affairs. Now it is my experience that such men, having entered their sixties, tend to be either over-hearty or on the cool and dry side. Though a very agreeable host, Sir John belonged to the cooler and drier ones. The last thing he would want to do would be to surprise a visitor; but that, without trying, is what Sir John did to me. To begin with, there he was, over 5,000 feet up in South Canterbury, New Zealand, living in a mid-Victorian English country house, gabled and substantially built of red brick, that might have been plucked out of the Acland estates in Devonshire. And not only that, for he was living there entirely alone, Lady Acland being in Singapore, staying, I think, with one of their sons; and if there was any domestic staff to keep that large house going, I saw no sign of it. True, one of his three sons, with a decorative wife and some children, was living in a newly-completed house, all very modern, just down below. This Mr and Mrs Acland came up to see us, and later, just before we left, we went down to visit them and to admire their house. But it was all a bit odd and surprising, though entirely agreeable.

Sir John himself surprised me by appearing to be so completely English in appearance, manner, speech, when in fact he was born and bred in New Zealand and educated at Christ's College. His father, Sir Hugh Acland, was also a New Zealander; he had a long and very distinguished career as a surgeon. His grandfather, John Barton Arundel Acland, a Harrow and Oxford man and a barrister, came out

to New Zealand with his close friend Tripp in 1855, and the pair of
them worked on established sheep farms to learn the business. They
moved up into the largely unexplored high country because all the
easier land had been already claimed. Mount Peel station came into a
rough-and-ready existence as early as 1856, and ten years later Acland
had built this impressive homestead, shortly afterwards adding an
attractive little church. He was able to combine the roles of benevolent
squire, enthusiastic radical and pious churchman. But his dream of
surrounding himself with a number of contented small farmers was
not realized, the huge and difficult high country estates not being
suitable for this style of cosy agriculture. Mount Peel survived, as we
have seen, but not without some hard times and an enforced reduction
of its original vast acreage. And indeed, Sir John, our host, told us how
there are neighbouring roads separating lands that ran five sheep to
the acre from poorer country that demanded five acres to a sheep. One
family interest that now paid handsome dividends to a visitor's eye
was its concern for importing and planting all manner of trees. We
even caught sight of our old Californian friends, the *sequoia*.

Putting himself hospitably at our disposal after lunch, Sir John ran
us out to a road where Jacquetta could start a walk, on which she
gathered mushrooms and a giant puff-ball and then, not without
pride in the achievement, found a way along a very obscure path down
through plantations back to the house. I had only to sit on the grass by
the road and do a paint, staring up at the mountains. But no doubt to
Sir John's surprise I decided to turn my back on them and look down
the road, which as it dropped away revealed a distant view of the
Canterbury plain, there in a haze of blue. I had done similar scenes at
home, after picnics on one or other of the Cotswold hills, from which
I could see the Midlands plain to the north. But I was more at ease
with Worcestershire and Gloucestershire than I was with South
Canterbury, and though I didn't do badly with the distant blue plain,
my foreground of dry grass and scrub was a dingy nothing. So this
was just another disappointing sketch. However, I have decided not
to offer any more examples of failure. They will exist but I shall keep
quiet about them. While my faults as an artist can be excused, for after

all I didn't begin until I was over 60, I have no excuse for being boring about them.

After tea we explored and admired the smart modern house of the younger Aclands, were collected by Mr Goode, and went off in style, Sir John's small granddaughter and her friend cantering their ponies beside our car. This good day's glorious weather was now breaking as we made our way back to Mount Possession. Recalling that substantial and enduring Acland homestead, I began to think about the men who must have built it, feeling sure that quite a number of skilled men and reliable labourers, mostly from Devon, must have been persuaded to leave England for New Zealand. The earliest Acland probably did this privately, but in museums I saw advertisements of the 1850's and 1860's aimed at God-fearing industrious artisans and farm-hands, offering them work and good prospects, especially in the Canterbury settlements. I told myself then how fortunate New Zealand had been, easily the most fortunate of all the old British colonies. In the earliest whaling days, some rough customers, probably deserters, must have arrived; and during the gold rush of the 1860's all manner of mining toughs must have come roaring in from Australia and California. But these were exceptional short periods. There had been no constant importation of riffraff, boozy remittance men, desperate types a jump ahead of the police, and the like. The wild Irish had mostly gone to New York and Boston, there to corrupt local politics; or to Australia, where they succeeded in keeping warm an anti-English feeling. It was the industrious God-fearing Anglicans and cautious hard-working Scots who settled in New Zealand.

But there was Samuel Butler, in many ways the oddest and in the end the most distinguished of all New Zealand immigrants. My thoughts turned naturally to him because this high country we were in now was also his chosen territory, first explored and then claimed by him. His old Mesopotamia homestead, a 'sod and cob cottage' in his time, might be said to be almost round the corner. Consider his oddity as an immigrant. After leaving Cambridge he was lay-reader (increasingly sceptical) to a London curate; then against his father's wishes, he tried to study art; and finally was packed off to New

Zealand. His qualifications for the exploration of new territory, for sheep farming, for property deals, were nil. Even his voyage out was strange, for he had originally booked a passage in the *Burmah* but then transferred to the *Roman Emperor*, which arrived safely whereas the *Burmah* sank and drowned everybody. We need not follow all his transactions in South Canterbury; it is sufficient to say that by the time he decided to go back home, only four years later, he had doubled his capital. (He arrived in 1860, left in 1864.) But though he had furnished his sod cottage with piano, books, pictures – no easy trick with bullock carts on hillside tracks – we are told he spent more and more time down in Christchurch, painting and exhibiting pictures, playing at concerts, writing for the local press, even making official speeches – and he was still only in his later twenties and a comparative newcomer. He seems to have been Christchurch's brash young all-rounder. His return to London did more to enlarge rather than to discourage his versatility. His books, with their originality and cheerful impudence, attracted more and more attention; he painted fairly successful pictures (one is in the Tate Gallery); and he might have made a musical reputation if he hadn't been so passionately certain that Handel was the greatest composer who ever lived. But he seems to have left his financial acumen behind in New Zealand with his twenties. He invested almost all the money he had made there, taking it away when it was paying him 10 per cent interest, in new Canadian enterprises and, as people used to say, lost his shirt. He was only able later to live in modest comfort in London and indulge in Victorian inexpensive travel because his father left him money and his writing brought him a small regular income. He remains, I feel sure, New Zealand's oddest immigrant, as well as being a notable influence – in ideas, manner, style – on no less a person than George Bernard Shaw.

So we returned to Mount Possession, to a welcome hot supper conjured up by smiling Mrs Dobbs, and to a Sunday evening of indifferent television interrupted or dismissed by cosy chat. Next morning was wet and misty. We had a rather vague engagement to visit a station further away and higher than Mount Peel, and everybody agreed it would be folly to go up there. After some complicated telephoning by Mrs Dobbs, the people at the other end – and I don't think I ever knew their names – were given the news. It was about this time, I fancy, that Pat Goode began playing his Mount Cook card. If the weather cleared, and he believed it would after lunch, then we might as well be on our way to Queenstown, where we had arranged to stay several days. But why not break our journey to Queenstown by spending the night at the Hermitage, that magnificent hotel, the pride of the South Island and the Tourist Hotel Corporation, and giving ourselves the chance of seeing Mount Cook National Park? But – and we had no map handy – would this be on the way to Queenstown? Surely, certainly, undoubtedly it would be, the reply came. That Mount Cook card, played again and again, began taking every trick.

We told Mrs Dobbs that if the weather cleared we would not be staying another night, and she said how sorry she was. Now in some situations I am still a closely observant man, and it seemed to me that the bright eye of Mrs Dobbs, at the very moment she received our announcement, brightened still more. I am not blaming her. Haven't I already set down my appreciation of and temporary devotion to Mrs Dobbs? But she has a lot on her plate, what with a husband mustering away up there in foul weather, three children travelling to and from school, and various people coming and going, and we at least were now getting off her plate. But not before lunch, which we ate in the grander (though less fascinating) out-of-kitchen style, for now she had two other guests – out from Christchurch: Mr Harper, Dalgety's chief manager there, and Mrs Harper, a calm and cultivated woman, whose talk I enjoyed. The rain and mist had gone, though the landscape was darkened by low clouds. Goodbyes were said and waved. Mount Possession had taught me absolutely nothing about running a large sheep station; I had learnt more watching Mrs Dobbs at the kitchen range; but I had enjoyed being there and was grateful – and still am – to have been its guest.

CHAPTER 6

On the way to Queenstown

There is a little gap in my memory of the very early part of our journey from Mount Possession. So I must first ask a question instead of making a definite statement. Was it then, travelling beneath a canopy of dark low cloud, that I first noticed a sky effect that I was to observe more than once later, a peculiar effect not without some psychological significance? Allow me to assume that I first noticed this effect there and then, so that I may describe it while I have it in mind. The dark, low cloud did not cover everything. Lower down still, just above the horizon, was a cloudless space, through which there came an intense white light, so intense, so incandescent, that it might have been coming from an invisible furnace. The total effect was not hopeful, suggesting that sunlight was on its way to rescue us from the cloud, though this may have been the truth of the matter. No, it was sinister, strangely menacing, suddenly revealing another and terrible aspect of the New Zealand scene. Some Nature god of the South Pacific, the same power that could without warning bring cold lashing storms out of these skies, was showing us his other face, warning us that we were deceiving ourselves if we thought we were in another Eden.

Even without the roof of cloud and the unearthly white light below or the sudden storms that seemed to come from another climate, I couldn't help feeling that whenever the sunlight vanished from these scenes, draining the colour out of them, then something vaguely sinister, something hostile to Man, crept into the atmosphere. Could

55

this partly explain the unusual friendliness of people here, all in the same boat and a long way from anywhere? Might it also explain – and I am guessing and stand to be corrected – that even when taking into account such disasters as long droughts, unexpected snowstorms, shocking falls in the prices of wool and meat, older New Zealanders, not the optimistic early settlers but their grandchildren, were liable to panic moods and measures? Just as if they had known deepdown all along that this place was too good to be true, that they were remote islanders building on false hopes, and that the sinister aspect of the scene whenever the sun left it offered them an urgent message?

The sky lightened as we went on and Mr Goode, brooding over the Hermitage (reported to be full up), took us by way of the townlets Geraldine and Fairlie into and through the fabled Mackenzie Country. I have two quite different reasons for bringing in the term 'fabled' here. The first and far more obvious is concerned with the James McKenzie who gave his name (in spite of the different spelling) to this region, though it appears now that he was not the first to explore it. He was a Highlander who went to Australia and then moved on to New Zealand in the earlier 1850's. He had land, this land, that he had claimed, but no stock, and apparently he decided to remedy this by sheep rustling, aided, the story runs, by a wonderfully clever dog. In April 1855 he was charged with stealing about 1,000 sheep from a South Canterbury station and was sent to prison for five years. He escaped twice but was soon recaptured. However, in January 1856 he was given a free pardon, having convinced the authorities that they had arrested and condemned the wrong man, he himself having been engaged simply to drive the missing sheep to Otago. Later in January 1856 he booked a return passage to Australia and then sailed out of history. But after some years, when nothing more was heard of him, he came sailing back – this time into legend. He and his wonderful dog were credited with extraordinary feats of cunning. The truth is, of course, that people must have legends and if necessary will make do with a dubious sheep-drover. More recently, as I suggested earlier, it is the Maori who have taken over the legendary, the fabulous, the romantic and glamorous, and no McKenzie, innocent or guilty, need apply. The fact remains, however, that with an *a* added to it his name still covers this region.

This brings me to the second and less obvious (though to me more important) reason why I used the term 'fabled'. As I passed through it that afternoon this Mackenzie Country seemed to me fabulously beautiful. It might have been the landscape of some rare happy dream. Possibly the autumnal time and the afternoon light conspired to favour it so that this was the scene in its most radiant hour. I don't know; I had never set eyes on it before, I never saw it again; and now, unless I am granted the freedom of the fifth dimension, I have no hope of ever seeing it again. But why did I let this marvellous landscape flow past me, bound for oblivion? Why – on a coarser note – didn't I stop the car and get out paper and paints? Partly because I am weak of will when sitting in a car hurrying towards an agreed destination. But also, I think, because the passing landscape I stared at must have had a semi-hypnotic effect upon me. Beyond the wide and darkish plain were mountains, catching the light, that might have been guarding the fields of Paradise. They didn't belong to this world at all. They were outside geography and history, politics and all fiscal arrangements. They had been shaped, coloured, illuminated, by angelic masters. They had peaks of pearl, gold and amethyst, rising above cerulean and sapphire shadows and final recesses of indigo. I ought to have said that the plain was deep as well as wide, so that these were no looming lumps of earth and rock but mountains that seemed far away, marbled and jewelled, iridescent and many-coloured, all along the horizon, hiding some other and better world from us. When they finally vanished, it was not the same afternoon but one that was darker and smaller, fit for peevish complaints.

These came when we turned north to bump, bounce and shudder over the 37 miles Hermitage-bound along the western shore of Lake Pukaki. It was indeed a vile road, though by now it may be much better for various lengths of it were under repair. Even Jacquetta, who combines intellectual and literary gifts with an astonishingly sweet temper (rare among clever women, in my experience), felt compelled to write in her notes: 'I felt sick and cross and told Mr Goode that his

Mount Cook scheme was a rotten one . . .' (But she apologized for that next morning.) We gave Lake Pukaki, which seemed to go on for ever, hardly a look, though perhaps an occasional glare. When at last we stopped outside the lights and imposing bulk of the Hermitage and Mr Goode dashed inside, to his consternation, even shame, he learnt that what they had already told him over the telephone was true – there was not the smallest bedroom vacant for us: the place was full. So Mr Goode had to take us and his fallen crest down the road to the new Glencoe, a very large motel. Our room there was rather small but ingeniously designed, with facilities, quite strange and fascinating to us, for making your own continental breakfast as well as early morning tea. Moreover, we had already arranged to dine at the Hermitage, where for the first time in New Zealand I felt I was surrounded by the rich and the grand. The dinner was good; the Alpine landscapes offered for sale in one of the smaller public rooms were terrible; I sneered at them before returning to Glencoe and the less rich, less grand – but all able to make their own continental breakfast.

The morning might have been newly minted for us, crisp and bright. Jacquetta noted (though I didn't) that Mount Sefton was gloriously gleaming, but Mount Cook and its 12,349 feet were not in sight. She went briskly off to the the foot of Mount Sefton, where she heard the deep rumblings of the fast-moving glaciers. (Afterwards she was able to show me the summit of Mount Cook, just to say I had seen it – though I am capable at a pinch, not for false glory but to avoid tedium, of saying I have seen something when I haven't.) Meanwhile, I sat down in front of Glencoe and worked like a madman for a few but exalted minutes, sketching a fierce little mountain that was glaring across the valley at me. This fellow – and I never learnt its name – was my meat. Oh – I can do a bad paint of snowy peaks and glaciers with the next man, who is always doing them, but I hadn't the inclination, the equipment, the technique, to do a good paint, so why bother about them? My little mountain, at that fairly early hour, demanded some biggish brushes loaded with ivory black and indigo (one rarely has a good excuse for indigo), and as I plied them at full speed I felt I was creating a master work. Of course I wasn't, but nobody can take away from me what I felt during those few minutes. Mount Cook might reach 12,349 feet, but I was up to 12,350.

We left for Queenstown about the middle of the morning. The road alongside Lake Pukaki was still rough going but didn't seem as bad now as it had done the evening before. The truth is of course that all of us exist in two different places at one and the same time. There is the place outside us, the one on the map, the solidly objective one; there is the place inside us, the one within the mind, the psychological place. (The essential self, once it understands the situation it is in, has some power of choice as to where it should live in this interior country of the mind and if necessary can move from a bad psychological place to a good one.) Many a man rich enough to own four beautiful houses cannot enjoy them because, in the interior country he carries around, he has chosen to exist in a slum or a miasmic swamp. We all have bad places in the mind, and the trick – not easy, I admit – is not to identify ourselves with them but to move out of them. I realize that this is *As-if* reasoning, the sort of thing that most philosophers pounce upon to denounce; but if we can remember to act upon it, then it will work in a rough-and-ready fashion and release us from much misery, which is something most philosophers cannot do. So while the road round Lake Pukaki was just the same as it had been the evening before, we found it endurable because we were now living in a much better psychological place.

I wish I could remember, in geographical terms, where we stopped for lunch; but I can't, not even after staring at two fairly large-scale maps. So here I am, at the other end of the earth, remembering this tiny sketch of a hamlet with affection but unable to give it a name. It consisted of a small tearoom, enclosed within a rose-garden, and a neighbouring general store: and that was all. If there were any houses near by, I never saw them; never a glimpse of one. Just the tearoom and the store, but also some extremely pleasant friendly women apparently in charge of everything. We ate sandwiches and scones (with jam and cream), and drank cold milk laced with whisky. This is a particularly good drink late at night, but there is nothing wrong with

it at about 1.20 p.m. on a warm day. After lunch, Jacquetta wandered
next door to see what they were selling there. She was so pleased with
the store and (her note) 'the very nice young woman' who was looking
after it, she came back to suggest that I should take a look at it, which
of course I did. It was a real store, containing almost everything that
sensible people – as distinct from those with more money than sense –
could want to support a satisfactory existence. So far, so good; but
now we came to *abracadabra*, illusion, the magical part. The nice
young woman had said to Jacquetta, 'The schoolchildren should meet
anyone so famous as your husband,' which made no sense to her and
none to me when she reported it, for there were no schoolchildren in
the store, none in the tearoom, none in the road outside so far as we
could see. So we dismissed this odd remark and I stayed a little longer,
exploring the darker corners of the store. Then, taking my leave, I
halted, dumb with amazement, in the doorway.

There, facing me in a compact group, were about 20 schoolchildren, magically transported from the unknown. There too was
their schoolmaster, who proceeded at once – just as if he and I had
already set it up between us – to introduce me and to tell the children
they could ask questions. They were, I fancy, mostly between 10 and
12 years of age, and were very shy. So was I, for that matter; and was
probably still gaping goggle-eyed at them. The only person who
wasn't shy was the schoolmaster, who was brisk and commanding
after the manner of his kind. (My father was a schoolmaster.) When
the questions finally came, they were almost always the same question
– *What was it like to write?* – or – *to be a writer?* – just as if repetition
didn't worry them because each child felt he or she was asking a
private question, the others ceasing to exist for a few moments. I
found it rather hard going and so, I suspect, did everybody else except
the schoolmaster, who continued to be brisk and commanding but
probably unwilling now to give any of us good marks. But I never had
time to explain to him that I was still lost in wonder at the inexplicable,
almost necromantic presence of these children, a class conjured out of
air. There may have been a moment – though I won't swear to this –
when I fancied that if I turned round I might discover that the store

The steam at Wairakei, North Island

Lake Taupo, North Island, as seen just outside our room

Man in the Mountains by Wong Sing Tai
*(By courtesy of the Trustees of the National Art Gallery
and Dominion Museum)*

Terrace Lands by Nugent Welch
*(By courtesy of the Trustees of the National Art Gallery
and Dominion Museum)*

and the tearoom had vanished. However, Jacquetta's note is more sensible than anything I am writing here: 'Somehow this little break represented the best of New Zealand.' True enough; well said; but there might have been a reference, however brief, to the magical transport facilities of the local education authorities.

Now in the middle of the afternoon we were in the Lindis Pass and Central Otago mountain country. Many people who will read this book may have seen these Otago mountains in a different season (ours was early autumn), in quite different weather, during another kind of day, without our hard bright light. If so, such readers must bear with me while I report what I saw and thought and felt on this last Wednesday in March. I can only describe my Otago mountains, not theirs. They had a very narrow range of colour, that afternoon, from yellow ochre to something between raw sienna and raw umber. Their texture suggested anything from a roughened bronze to a well-worn and weathered light fur-coat. To declare their aspect unfriendly would be an understatement. Apparently they had heard some vague rumours about a species like ours, making a little dust below, and were not waiting for us to go just as quickly as we had arrived. They glared at us implacably. It was impossible to imagine any human hopeful enterprise in the region they commanded. This was the landscape that came to my mind when, as a boy, I read the wilder and more sinister tales of the *Arabian Nights*. Now and again their slopes burst into fantastic out-croppings of rock, and these might have been all that was left of monstrous idols worshipped by some lost race of giants. (And perhaps all the tussocks we had seen were among their daintier vegetables, their asparagus.) Just because I believe that we live in a mystery, not to be solved in labs, I admit to being a rather superstitious man. So if I were a South Islander, maybe a Canterbury plainsman rich in herds and harvests or a prosperous Dunedin merchant, pleased with myself and not without a taint of *hubris*, I would not only touch wood but would also remember these mountains of Central Otago, waiting here in the middle of the Island. Perhaps I might even take another look at them on a bright, hard afternoon like this. But just one odd glimpse before we leave the region – it was of two men about to play golf. I could barely trust my eyes: they might have been fixing up a game on the moon.

Those ramparts of a dead land having gone, I could now look down through my other window and see a glitter of water, orchards, white bungalows. Soon we ran into the green dusk of gorges and seemed to hear the thunder of impatient rivers. There were some pinkish cliffs that were curiously ugly. They were the victims of the old dredging and sluicing processes of gold-mining, once it had left behind the original pick-shovel-tinpan method. Earth and anything soft had been washed away. The natural faces of the cliffs weren't there any more; they were distorted now by the warts, clumps, knobs of remaining hard rock. There was melancholy as well as ugliness in these ruined cliff-faces; now they hadn't any gold to offer, they hadn't anything to offer; they reminded me of some little industrial ghost towns of my youth, vacant and sad after enterprise, greed and distant shareholders had done with them.

As we were in no great hurry to reach Queenstown, we agreed that Mr Goode, for ever concerned to show us everything, should make a short detour to take us into Arrowtown. We entered it along its famous tree-shaded avenue. The trees here, all of them English, were planted and then carefully protected in the later 1860's; and to show that the evil principle is at work at all times and in all places – it has been murderous lately in England – it was seriously proposed, just after the First War, that *these trees should be cut down*. So now, progress having been challenged and halted, with the trees half-a-century older and bigger, under their long archway of mingled foliage we glided into Arrowtown – and I say 'glided' because if there is one driver who knows how to pay respect to a marvellous avenue it is Mr Goode.

All was very quiet, indeed somnolent. The gold that had once packed the place with miners, roaring in and out of its taverns, had vanished, but only to reappear in so may of its bright leaves. At each side of its uneven main street there were some of the original buildings of the early 1860's, when wood and stone quickly took over from the canvas and calico of the first tents and shanties. There was a good little museum and, in a space just outside it, an exhibition of the vehicles of the gold rush days. Indeed, almost everything that catches the eye along that street, bars, stores, odd little shops, is intended to remind one of those days. It is as if the gold rush went through the place like a huge thundering tide, leaving behind, so many quaint shells on the shore, these bar names and shop signs once so gleefully hailed by the miners. (Here I ought to add that we paid Arrowtown another visit later.) But while Arrowtown might easily have been a tourist-trap, I felt that it wasn't. It had a quiet dignity of its own, because, I imagine, it didn't exist simply to exhibit and sell souvenirs of its gold-mining past. It still served its own community.

There is a distinction here of some importance. Because we fell in love with an old house and its large garden in the very pleasant village of Alveston, we happen to live only two or three miles from Stratford-upon-Avon. Now there must be thousands of people, perhaps hundreds of thousands, who think of this town as one of the supreme tourist-traps of the world, just selling Shakespeare day and night. And certainly it has an ever-increasing tourist trade, and the charges for admission into the various places associated with Shakespeare enable the Birthplace Trust, which does not exist to make a profit, to keep the buildings in good repair and their gardens both tidy and blooming. But surprising as it may seem, probably two out of every three Stratfordians would be indignant if it was suggested to them they were earning a living out of Shakespeare or indeed owed anything to him at all. They would point out at once that Stratford is an important market town that also supports various light industries. (I think sometimes that many of them don't even *like Shakespeare*.) In short, the town serves its own regional community. I am not pretending that it would not be worse off if all the tourists disappeared. But it would still be there, not doing too badly. It is a fact that at all holiday times, except in the dead of winter, the town is crowded with families who arrive on day trips from Coventry and Birmingham. Now these people aren't interested in Shakespeare – they don't, so to speak, go near him – they go on the river or stare at it or feed the swans; they sit about or play with their children in the public gardens; they even crowd the pavements – though God knows why – of the shopping streets, as if they had just landed from a ship and not a motor-coach or train. And all this, like the attitude of so many of the townspeople, is far removed from tourism and tourist-traps. So the place has a healthy and varied life of its own, nothing to do with package tours and Americans and Japanese and Germans and tip-hunger. And this would have pleased Shakespeare, who was not only a great poet and a great dramatist but also (and this will disgust some of his critics) a sensible man – and a good Stratfordian.

Some such thoughts as these were passing through my mind as I stood, staring about me, in the main street of Arrowtown, after deciding that it had a life of its own, though not one marked by hustle and bustle and stress. But a few minutes later I was thinking about films. I don't spend much time these days thinking about them, even though my only son, Tom, is now a very successful film editor and sends us picture postcards from 'locations' that may be anywhere in Western Europe or America. What had happened was that we had sauntered almost to the end of the main street, with Mr Goode and his car 'tailing' us, and then I had turned round to see if anything was happening in Arrowtown. Nothing was; and then I told myself that it looked like a film set, not in use because the producer, the director, and three writers were shouting one another down over the script.

So then, without forgetting Arrowtown, I began thinking about films and didn't stop when we got into the car. I asked myself why I had never seen a big feature film about the Otago gold rush of the early 1860's. It was ridiculous, especially now when the search for new subjects and locations appeared to be desperately urgent. To begin with, the 1860's was visually a promising period. Then hadn't about 22,000 men and their camp followers invaded this region? Some had come from the diggings in Australia and California; there must have been plenty of rough and tough types; with real riffraff moving in too – like Bully Hayes. A lot of them flocked into what was afterwards Arrowtown, looking for a change of grub, booze and women to marry. (Yes to marry, often within a week of their arrival. One man, despairing of new feminine help, asked Dunedin to send him the ugliest woman in town, and even she was married off in a fortnight.) Some of the miners were armed, though there were few if any of the gunfights associated, much too often in my opinion, with the American West. But is this a weakness of the New Zealand scene? Once past the age of ten, haven't we all had more than we want of *bang-bang-bang*?

Hardly conscious of the magnificent scenery we were passing on our way to Queenstown, I said to myself that it isn't more and more gun-play, bloodier and bloodier wounds and deaths, we need now on our screens. What we want are picturesque backgrounds, dramatic settings, that are no longer stale and so many scenic clichés. I have affectionate memories of my old holiday-ground, Arizona, which I know from Tombstone in the south to the hopelessly overdone Monument Valley in the north; but I would be glad not to see any of it again in a film. Moreover, simply considered as a setting for an adventure film, this Otago country makes the American South-West look like tuppence. It has everything – peaks and precipitous slopes, lakes and swift rivers and mysterious gorges, a choice of sun-baked plains and icy winds and sudden snowfalls, according to the chosen season – really, the lot! And then there are those sinister Central Otago mountains. To bring them in – and I saw them as essential – I even began sketching to myself the very rough genesis of a film plot – *A Stark and Spine-chilling Story of Robbery, Pursuit and Revenge in a Remote and Terrible Wasteland! ! !*

While I could supply better names if I had a contract, let us say that Smith, Jones and Brown are partners in the Otago gold rush. The time then is the 1860's and with any luck we may get a peep or two at or under a crinoline. These three strike it lucky, and they draw lots to decide which of them shall look after the gold before they take it south to be weighed. (All three are idiots, but then this is an adventure film, not aimed at highbrows at the Venice Festival.) It is Brown, no honest Kiwi but a Californian or Australian, who can't resist the temptation to sneak off with the gold in the middle of the night. The poor fool decides to go north, perhaps in the hope of selling the gold to an Anglican clergyman in Christchurch, and in any event avoiding the awkward questions he might have to face if he went south. (Some muttered interior monologue here – clumsy I know, but you can't have everything.) Moreover, in his haste and the dark he leaves an obvious back trail, which Smith and Jones (a comic Welshman until we get him into those mountains) immediately discover as soon as the sun is up. They set out in urgent pursuit of Brown and their share – probably his share too – of the gold. (Do horses, bullocks or just feet come into this? I don't know; but after all I am now giving this away: no contract, not even a percentage.) Brown learns – never mind how – that Smith and Jones, feeling murderous by this time, are hot on his trail. He hopes to escape by taking to the mountains, those same Central Otago mountains, remember; and they can be either covering themselves with snow or baking in hellish sunlight, just as the director pleases. Smith and Jones (no longer playing for comedy) are close behind him. The next three or four reels, all breathtaking stuff, give us the film of adventure at its best, and they put New Zealand on the film producers' map.

And that is where I stopped, not because I couldn't invent anything else but because I had already caught the blue gleam of Lake Wakatipu, had noticed the darkish foliage of the tall evergreens and the delicate yellowing leaves of various smaller trees, and then found we were surrounded by the neat bungalows of outer Queenstown. Enough of film nonsense! Derek Morris and our itinerary had set us down here for four nights, so if for any reason we didn't like the place, then we were about to run clean out of luck.

CHAPTER 7

At Queenstown

It seemed at first: that is, we were running clean out of luck. This is what happened. Even Mr Goode felt we had had enough of sight-seeing for one day, so instead of showing us Queenstown he took us straight through it – or as straight as you can go through Queenstown, which has a detouring style – on and up to our hotel. It was out of the town, which was all right, but it was also at the end of a dusty, bad road, which was not all right. If it expected to live up to its advertising, which probably hypnotized Derek in some ecstasy of long-distance phoning, then one could only say that as yet it was half finished. So for example the splendid view hadn't been delivered. The garden, in which one could sit to enjoy the view when it arrived, hadn't been brought into existence yet. The spacious grounds might have been there, but at the moment they were somewhere beneath the raw clutter of a building site. The terraced swimming-pool was small, dark, bristling with electrical gear because something wasn't working, so that it suggested an invention out of science fiction. There didn't seem to be enough staff – they were 'doubling in brass' as the Americans say – but then perhaps the rest of the staff was bringing along the view and the garden and another swimming-pool. Not that the people already working there were inadequate for it was even more under-guested than under-staffed. I don't remember passing anybody along our corridor. Perhaps you had to live in the North Island, like Derek, to believe in this pearl of the South Island.

But I have grumbled and jeered long enough. After our first sharp disappointment, coming at the end of a long day, we soon settled down, making the best of what we had, even though that bad dusty road remained a nuisance. It is only fair to add that if we were making the best of it, so were the members of the staff in their various changing roles. I never saw any long or sour faces. Rather to our surprise, the hotel dining-room attracted people in the town as a restaurant, which suggested that Queenstown, for all its charm, is no place for a gourmet. The food could be good one night and bad the next, as if there were no dependable professionals in the kitchen but only amateurs who could work well only in the glow of inspiration. (The hotel speciality was home-baked bread, served still hot at dinner and a terrible temptation to Jacquetta.) I gathered from somebody in the business that hotel staffs in New Zealand were employed under strict trade union rules, with guaranteed working hours and wages. Chefs, I was told, were well paid and did very nicely, thank you. Diners at the mercy of the chefs seemed to me to be not so happily situated. No union existed to protect their palates. If you were given an inedible steak, as I was one night there, you were not at liberty to hurl the wretched thing through the kitchen hatch together with a few curses. Having been brought up in an industrial city, where so many people had been over-worked and under-paid, I have always sympathized with the trade union movement. But it has one weakness, namely, that while it insists upon guaranteed hours and wages it doesn't, unlike the medieval guilds, also insist upon good workmanship. Both in Britain and New Zealand it wields enormous power but it is not really independent and creative; there is something negative about it even now, something shifting and anomalous, not really accepting full responsibility, too often quite indifferent to the enterprise that is employing its men. (Once at the first night of one of my plays, the all-important final curtain failed to come down at the exact right moment, creating a dreadful hiatus; and this was because the union man, who should have given the signal for its descent, was still busy working out the time-sheet for his fellow union men.) And I can't help feeling that if New Zealand chefs have guaranteed hours and wages, they should first be compelled to pass an examination, and quite a stiff examination too, with marks deducted for inedible steaks.

Apparently we were in Queenstown at just the right time, this being autumn. I take this from *The Companion Guide to the South Island* by Mr Errol Braithwaite, who is so much more eloquent about Queenstown than I can be – after all he is a New Zealander and 30 years younger than I am – that I take the liberty of quoting him:

> But autumn is my favourite time, when the worst of the holiday crush is over, and the Queenstown people have time to stop and be charmingly helpful and friendly. The place seems to recover its good humour, and your days are filled with glorious colour, and the air is so good you can almost taste it; and you can step out of your room onto a balcony overlooking the lake, and see, across the water, the early snow on the Remarkables pink with fading sunlight, or mirror-bright in the smile of a full moon. And the smoke from the houses in the little town rises thin and blue in the shadow of the great hill, and the atmosphere is crisp and chill. . . .

Many of these delightful effects were denied us. Even arriving as we did at the end of March I think we must have been at least a month too early. Our days there in fact were quite warm, and the town still appeared to have plenty of visitors, though I agree that its people were 'charmingly helpful and friendly', but then so were people everywhere else too. And I think there are various reasons, at different levels, for this helpfulness and friendliness. One is that New Zealanders, unlike so many of the English, enjoy plenty of living-space and so don't feel the all-these-people stress and pressure. Another reason, on a lower and less conscious level, comes from their sense of remoteness, of being on an island lost in a huge ocean where the next stop is the Antarctic wilderness. Finally, there are those occasional moments when the landscape itself suddenly seems sinister and menacing, and such moments bring people to a feeling of a common destiny and so encourage them to be helpful and friendly.

But I could be wrong. Unlike politicians and editors, I am often wrong.

We split up during our first morning at Queenstown. Jacquetta, who has a nose for a good thing, found the beautiful public gardens above the lake and wrote letters there. I shouldered my painting gear through the trees near the hotel until I discovered a view of the town across the water. I did a rather careful unexciting paint, being rather too anxious, I fancy, to avoid the coloured-picture postcard style that Queenstown itself, as distinct from its magnificent surrounds, tends to encourage. Early in the afternoon we explored the town together. It was fullish but not unpleasantly crowded, as it must be during the summer and winter holiday seasons. It was just beginning to retreat from being a resort into being a sensible little town again. I took a fancy at once to the lake end of its main street, just because it was closed to traffic and you could potter around, looking at its shops, feeling at ease. (The more and more I see of these traffic-free shopping streets, the more and more I enjoy them and applaud them. I would keep all cars out of the lower end of Bond Street tomorrow.) But though this is a nice little town, with an Alpine flavour and many reminiscences of its origin as a gold-mining centre, I feel it owes almost everything to its neighbours: to the gorges and splendours of the gold rivers, the Arrow and the Shotover; to the chameleon heights, 7,000 feet or so, of the Remarkables; and to the long reaches, 52 miles altogether and often ultramarine from its great depth, of its mysterious Lake Wakatipu, which rises and falls several inches every few minutes as if a vast monster might somehow be still breathing down in its darkness. In its earliest days, Queenstown depended entirely on the lake for its supplies, which came by boat from Kingston at the southern end of Lake Wakatipu; and there are grim tales of famine when supplies had failed, and of starving, half-crazy miners being kept at gun point from looting some newly-arrived boat. And before that, as we shall see, this same Lake Wakatipu keeps rising and falling, gleaming and winking, through some of the sagas of the earliest settlers, years before there was a Queenstown. And even when there was one, a photograph of 1866 cannot show us a tree in sight. Now it is a leafy, little town; but I

repeat, owing almost everything to its setting. If it should turn into a
relentless tourist-trap, then I hope Lake Wakatipu would rise and fall
faster and start some angry bubbling.

Later in the afternoon we called at Douglas Badcock's studio. He
had been told we were around and had phoned me at the hotel that
morning. We took tea with the Badcocks, and they dined with us the
following evening. For the benefit of the British and American readers,
I must explain that Douglas Badcock is a landscape painter. In his own
New Zealand he enjoys great popularity among ordinary people,
which means that he is not liked at all by those who feel they are
extraordinary people, and this may also mean that he can be judged
fairly only by an extra-extraordinary person – ME of course (grammar
or no grammar, it has to be 'me'). A note by Jacquetta, after our visit
to the Badcock studio, can be used to open the discussion: 'Jack
surprised me by his admiration for Mr Badcock's over-dramatic and
sometimes near-vulgar oils, landscapes, especially peaks, snowy and
otherwise. One of a broken-down waggon the only picture I really
liked – but the technical skill is remarkable.'

There are several points to be made here. To begin with, I think
Jacquetta was looking at these landscapes through English eyes. This
is what I did, quite unconsciously, when I painted my *gouaches* of the
actual New Zealand scene. I simply could not help toning everything
down, seeing the landscapes through a familiar English haze that
wasn't there. Badcock's bold oils were New Zealand country set down
in a direct New-Zealanderish fashion. 'This is how it is round here,'
they shouted. There was no obvious subjective element – and most
modern art is highly subjective or a mere bunch of tricks – but there is
a sense in which Badcock's boldest landscapes are wholly subjective
because they represent a point of view. Let me put it this way. A lot of
contemporary painters, bang in the movement, are trying to tell us,
though too often in a private language, how wonderful they are, how
critical, how sensitive, how much they suffer. But Badcock isn't
trying to tell us how wonderful he is, what courage and insight into
life he has. A modest man and a passionate lover of Nature, he is
summoning all his resources to glorify, in a downright Kiwi style, the

New Zealand scene in all its variety, drama and majesty. And to do this is to be an artist, however far out of fashion he may be.

Not to worry! – this book isn't going to turn into art criticism. But it happens that Douglas Badcock was the only New Zealand painter I talked with at some length, especially during our dinner and immediately afterwards, when he was more at ease and more forthcoming than he had been in his studio. Again, the situation he was in aroused my attention. As I was to discover more than once, he was admired and perhaps over-praised by one lot of people, more or less the general public, and was sniffed at and even abused by the artistic set, partly influenced by – and resenting – his popularity. Many of these sneerers, I fancy, imagine that what Jacquetta referred to as the 'over-dramatic' and 'sometimes near-vulgar' elements in Badcock's landscapes were deliberately brought in to please the crowd. I believe this to be quite wrong. They were there to please himself, an honest expression of what he felt about the scenes he was painting.

In my time as a writer I have been ponderously admonished by very solemn critics (Herbert Read, for one) for crowd-pleasing by going down to a cheerful knockabout vulgar level, and what such critics didn't understand is that here they were dealing with a robust and broadly-based personality who occasionally wanted to enjoy himself on that level, whether the crowd would like it or lump it. Indeed, I have always gone to work with the idea that as it is I who will have to take all the time and trouble, then what is in hand will have to please me, be what I want to do, without bothering about what some mysterious 'they' may want. As a matter of fact, as I have pointed out to many a group of publishers, theatre managers, film producers, this 'they' who must be given what they want don't know what they want until they get it, so why aim at a target that isn't there? Finally, a word to the critical young, determined not to enjoy anything that silly old Aunt Flo enjoys. Popularity proves nothing, one way or the other. Terrible plays and films have been popular but Shakespeare has pleased more crowds than they ever have. For several decades after his death, Dickens was dismissed as a mere popular novelist (see Leslie Stephen's patronizing and almost contemptuous account of him in our *Dictionary of National Biography* – a shocking job!) by critical opinion of course, not by the public; and now later critical opinion has decided that Dickens is one of the greatest novelists of his or any other time. So my advice is – don't take popularity into account; there are too many traps along that path; try some other and surer approach.

But not only have I just been indulging in egoism and egotism, I have been pushing the reader along a false trail, which often happens when the arts are confused. Badcock's bold and almost brash style was not adopted as a crowd-pleaser. He has gone all over the place in his caravan, a New Zealander excitedly discovering New Zealand and all the wealth that Nature has lavished on the country, and telling us in paint often at the top of his voice. It is a deep and impassioned Love of Nature, not the subtle potentialities of painting (this may come later) that stirs in his roots. This was clear throughout our talk after dinner. He was furiously against anything that threatened the natural scene. More industrial development would bring more money, and if there was more money about, then a popular painter like Badcock could probably double or treble his income. But he wanted none of this. He shared with passion our feeling that New Zealand should identify itself with the quality of life, not mere quantity, that it should not become another over-populated, over-polluted, rat-race course, that it should remain a place where a man could breathe, could be quiet and rest, could open himself to the beauty and variety of the magnificent natural scene.

He had made his home in Queenstown for the past 25 years – though not of course without spending much time away from it on painting trips – but now he felt – and I quote – 'it was ruined'. Evidently he saw in Queenstown another victim of the corrupting influence of tourism, and here I feel inclined to disagree with him, for it seems to me that Queenstown isn't primarily a 'tourist attraction' but simply a South Island holiday resort, not in my opinion the same thing. On the other hand, I am in entire agreement with him about the corrupting influence of tourism in general, of which I had seen a great deal more than he had. In our affluent societies, we are now busy all over the world turning the substance of life into catalogued shadows of it, transforming like evil sorcerers real living into vicarious ghost-living. We offer what other races or our ancestors acclaimed as the triumphant marvels of their age, as so many possible 'tourist attractions', most to satisfy the idle curiosity of people who genuinely acclaim nothing and only know the pettiest triumphs. In this deadly race from something to nothing, from rich reality to ghostland, the Americans – the supreme tourists – are easy winners. New Zealand should be a place for travellers to visit, to observe, to wonder at and to admire, and should refuse to turn itself into a cynical mess of package tours and 'tourist attractions' to be given an approving tick on the programme or yawned at while waiting for the next hot meal. This is a country that should preserve a sturdy, independent, rewarding life of its own, and not put it into pawn for more and more dollars.

The day that followed the Badcock dinner was more Jacquetta's than it was mine, so I shall steal her notes, just as she roughly set them down:

'Went to the Nurse Cavell Bridge on the Shotover River. While Jack painted a stretch of the river with wide shingle banks, I walked the Moonlight Track well up on the lower slopes of the mountain. A quite perfect walk in perfect weather. The willows with their yellow arrowheads sparkling against a deep blue sky. The dead Lombardy poplar with its silvery perpendicular tracery – ditto. Marvellous views along the Shotover Gorge, with the pleasant soft bridle-path running beside lines of poplar, already part yellow. Jack not pleased with his paint.'

I wasn't pleased with my paint because what I needed for that tremendous scene were oils and not *gouaches*, a canvas four times the size of my paper, several days instead of a couple of hours, and more talent.

To return to my wife:

'At 2 p.m. I boarded the *Earnslaw*, 61-year-old "Queen of the Lake" for the Walter Peak station. (She can do 18 knots, emitting a bushy cloud of black smoke from her tall, dirty red funnel.) A tourist trip, but the numbers small. Wiles (?), an English millionaire, so they say, had intended to turn Walter Peak into a great tourist centre, but only got as far as doing up the homestead. Some of the rooms are furnished with (rather good) wax models – girls at the piano, grandma in bed, etc. A very pleasant atmosphere. Apparently no fear of visitors stealing the many small objects lying about the house. Cheered by the prettiness of a fair-sized ginko tree: perhaps mine will equal it some day. Took acorns from the huge English oak to plant at Kissing Tree. Display of sheep-penning by (I think) son of the house. The dog a border collie – his specialist job being that of "eye dog" – silent and enormously concentrated.'

Meanwhile, equally silent and concentrated, I was looking for books in that pleasant traffic-free shopping street. Wilkinson's Pharmacy was obviously the place. After all, if you have to go to a hairdresser's for tobacco, then why not a pharmacy for books? I don't know how good the pharmaceutical department was but they had an enticing stock of New Zealand books, which were what I wanted. I was not going to take the books I bought away with me; our baggage was sufficiently heavy already; so the good lady who was looking after me began parcelling up my purchases to send them by post to England. Unfortunately there were certain significant weights she seemed to be aiming at, so that when I decided on buying another book, then the whole parcelling process had to begin all over again. However, she showed no impatience, and as I detest making up parcels I regarded her with wonder and awe. I didn't realize then that my turn to be patient would come later. It took two-and-a-half months for those books from Wilkinson's Pharmacy, Queenstown, to reach me here in Alveston, Warwickshire.

(When the books did reach me and I read the first three chapters of F. W. G. Miller's *Golden Days of Lake Country*, I changed my mind about a New Zealand film. The gold-miners of the 1860's can be ignored until a great historic film is based on the exploits, adventures, tribulations, courage and endurance of the early settlers of the 1850's in this Lake Wakatipu region. Those were the men, whether pious English gentlemen or stalwart Highlanders! They were better men than the gold-miners, often greedy and dubious, and perhaps better men, only wanting to raise sheep in new country, than most of those we have known in this century. Searching for unclaimed pastures, they improvised rafts to navigate the mysterious long lake; they lowered bullocks and carts down precipices. And when they had climbed mountains and descended into unknown valleys, had frozen or collapsed from the heat, and had at last claimed all their pastures, their work was not half-done and further ordeals had to be faced. The law demanded that within a given time these newly-claimed lands had to be raising sheep. So now great mobs of sheep had to be herded over the mountains and the precipices, ferried across lakes and rivers, suffering icy winds or blistering sunlight. And some of the settlers brought wives and families as well as herds of bewildered beasts; and they built huts and promptly held religious services in them; and so created remote outposts of mid-Victorian civilization, which in spite of the prejudices and limitations we snigger at now, somehow produced such remarkable men. In a recent book about the 1850's, *Victoria's Heyday*, I had followed men of this sort to the triumphs of sheer courage and the bitter shambles of the Crimean War, to the incredible marches and endurance tests of the Indian Mutiny, and now here they were again, displaying the same fortitude and determination so that they could raise sheep on these remote hardly-won pastures. And if ever New Zealand creates an ambitious historical film, these early Otago settlers are the men it should honour. In the meantime we could all stop sniggering at the mid-Victorians.)

Back to Queenstown for our last evening there. As my painting record so far has been largely darkened by disappointment and melancholy self-criticism, I want to improve it a little by indicating one tiny triumph, belonging to this evening. Mr Goode, who never on any occasion failed to be on hand when we wanted him, took us after tea across a bridge and then along a road that ran between the lake and the Remarkables. (There is to me something very Dickensian about that name for a range of mountains. Perhaps Lake Wakatipu ought to have been the Inimitable.) We didn't go far along that road. I saw a possible quick sketch; Jacquetta saw a possible quick walk; Mr Goode pulled up at the side of the road. There was a nice light,

Storm in the Gorge by John Weeks
*(By courtesy of the Trustees of the National Art Gallery
and Dominion Museum)*

Towards Wairakei by R. J. Waghorn
*(By courtesy of the Trustees of the National Art Gallery
and Dominion Museum)*

Lower Hollyford Valley by Douglas Badcock

Droving Sheep, Wairarapa, by D. R. Neilson

caught somewhere between late afternoon and early evening. The landscape had simplified itself for me. Within quarter of an hour I had finished my sketch, certainly to my satisfaction, and while I don't say it is anything to boast about, I do suggest it marks a turning point in the *gouache* history of this visit. From now on there would be fewer disappointments, even a modest triumph or two. Perhaps Wakatipu, no ordinary lake, helped to change the luck.

I think it was this same evening, actually our last in Queenstown, that the young man and I hatched a successful plot between us. This young man – was his name Robertson? – seemed to be the hotel's Admirable Crichton, popping up in all departments. The more enterprising young try everything now to look different, so that we have professional footballers whose appearance suggests concert pianists of 1910; and Robertson, as I feel I must call him, had decided to look like a more youthful Mephistopheles, though he was in fact an amiable and obliging chap. Catching him in his receptionist role, I leant across the counter and whispered, 'Do you like this piped music we have all the time?' He replied, 'No, I hate it.' Finding a certain piquancy in tempting Mephistopheles, I continued, 'So do I. You know how to turn it off – um? Well then, let's not have any more of it tonight. Off for once, eh?' The plot was hatched. And that night we dined without the damnable accompaniment of canned music.

I was sorry but not surprised that this American canned and piped-in music had invaded New Zealand, where I had heard it in planes, airports, hotel lounges and dining-rooms, but not, I think, in banks, stores, garages, in almost all public places, as one does in America itself. But give it time – and not even much – and soon this aural treacle will be dripping down innumerable Kiwi walls. It represents, as many things do now, the easy victory of commercial interests over mere inertia. After all, have the public – as distinct from managements – ever demanded this piped-in music? I doubt if anybody has ever entered a restaurant, hotel, store, airplane, and cried 'Where's the background mood music? Turn it on at once.' People in general have never asked for it. All they have done is passively to accept it, as they accept so many things they shouldn't accept, from nuclear bombs upwards or downwards. On the other hand, there are some of us who detest this nauseating stuff and try hard on occasion to get it switched off. Now if nobody eagerly demands it while my friends and I are passionately and furiously against it, then it should go. If it stays, we are no longer living in free societies.

Nor is that all. We should ask ourselves why managements in more and more places go to the trouble and expense of piping in this music-that-isn't music, never intended to be listened to properly. What are they up to? What's the idea? Are they simply trying to create a pleasant atmosphere to please their patrons? Some of them, probably many of them, still innocent and low-down in the scale of management, sincerely believe that this is what they are doing, every time they switch on the dim, treacly sound. But the root idea is very different. What we have here, as many a formidable board of directors must have realized, is part of the vast commercial plot against thought. Like so much of the most expensive and successful advertising, this canned pineapple-juice sound, with its sentimental associations, is also manipulating the unconscious of the consumers. Then haziness and muzziness, a feeling that all will be well without any sharp judgments being made, creep into their conscious minds. It is now far easier to delude, humbug, cheat the customers, and they will spend more money carelessly, even rashly, without quite realizing that *Moon River* and *Smoke Gets In Your Eyes*, together with 40 muted strings, have been successfully at work on them. Up, by all means, with real music, demanding close attention, and down, down, down with this canned piped-in background music!

If, on the Saturday morning, we were a bit late leaving Queenstown for Dunedin, it was probably my fault. Without knowing what I was up to, I may have done some lingering and stalling. Now this is very unusual for me, because I am the one who wants to move on to the next place. I amused myself once dividing people into peasants and tinkers. The peasants want to stay in one place, if they like it at all, and have a deep-seated desire to acquire a piece of it. They tend to be acquisitive and possessive but are able to build up civilizations. The tinkers are the restless types, who don't much care about owning anything but do want to be on the move, never making the best of one place and always tending to believe that the next town will be much better. I have always been a tinker, though perhaps now something of a tamed tinker, so any loitering before getting away, trying the next town, isn't my usual style at all. So how do I explain this Saturday morning? I think the truth is that I had come to like Queenstown and might have welcomed another few days in it, whereas, without really knowing anything about Dunedin, I was reluctant to go there, moved by a vague feeling that I would take a dislike to the place when I did get there. But my intuitive powers, the subject of an occasional boast, certainly weren't working that morning. However, though I was hopelessly wrong about Dunedin, I really had enjoyed our stay in Queenstown and left it with genuine regret.

CHAPTER 8

At Dunedin

If a man can be said to drive a car proudly, then Mr Goode drove us proudly into Alexandra, as if lunch there would be a rare treat. It is a pleasant little town, on a plain of its own, famous for its apricots and a Blossom Festival every September. It has the lowest rainfall in the country, but then it has two rivers and the great Manorburn Dam as its neighbour. Apparently it is crowded out with sportsmen and holiday-makers in winter and spring, but now in early autumn it was very quiet. Its oddest feature, which must be one of the South Island's best talking-points, is an enormous clock on the cliff-face across the river, and as its hour and minute hands are 13 feet and 18.6 feet respectively it is clearly visible by day and obligingly illuminated at night, so it is hardly worth giving an Alexandra man a gold presentation watch on retiring. Now at a majestic royal pace, Mr Goode conveyed us to the entrance of a splendid new motel-cum-hotel where the manager was a friend of his. The manager greeted us warmly and made us feel important, which is something we all like to feel at times. (One reason why our vast modern cities seem so frustrating and grim to most people is that they make those people feel less and less important. Even the old slums were better in this respect than the towers of flats that have replaced them, ant-hills in which nobody can feel, as I once heard a little girl say, 'in the importance'.) This genial clever manager immediately led us to the bar, to try an aperitif or two before lunch. This had not happened to us since we left Waitomo, and we were not even staying in this hotel. I have an idea that we had a good lunch, but then I would not hesitate to suppress any rising doubts. Incidentally, in the bar there was a very sociable man from Dunedin who wanted to stand a further round of drinks and offered to take us round the city in a day or two? Were these favourable omens at Alexandra beginning to make me feel I might have been wrong earlier to suspect this visit to Dunedin? The only honest reply is that I don't remember.

Indeed, I remember very little about the journey from Alexandra to Dunedin, no scenery being noted and admired; but I do recall that it seemed very roundabout and to take longer than I had anticipated. What I do remember all too well, for it is charged with melancholy, was our parting from that de-luxe driver of drivers, Pat Goode, at the entrance to the Southern Cross hotel in the muddled-middle of Dunedin. He had been with us ever since Mount Possession, had been perfect on all occasions, and we felt rather lost and sad after we had shaken hands and he had driven away. Our Derek-instructions, which of course were awaiting us, were that if we needed a driver we had to ring a certain garage, which was almost like exchanging a friend for a computer. As the Southern Cross wasn't new, it hadn't been designed only to accommodate midgets travelling with a toothbrush and miniature pyjamas; so we had room for ourselves, our possessions and a visitor or two. But we were back with the familiar old-style receptionists, found everywhere in the United Kingdom, that is, girls who while being reasonably polite, regard fat elderly men, obviously married too, with less interest than they would a stray cat. (It is only in the West of Ireland that very pretty girls smile at you across the reception counter as if they were welcoming a favourite uncle.) However, not only did we have space but we were fairly high up too and could easily reach the restaurant (not bad) on the top floor.

Further Derek-instructions included a suggestion rather than a demand that we should get in touch with Miss Shona McFarlane, journalist and artist, who was the Dunedin representative (unpaid) of the QE II Arts Council. So I telephoned her and asked her to dine with us if she happened to be free that evening. She was and she did.

And this proved to be the most rewarding telephone call of our whole visit. By the time she had been offered and had cheerfully accepted a pre-dinner drink, say, under five minutes, it was clear to us that she was an attractive and energetic person, bubbling with enthusiasm, and with many friends and a wide acquaintance in Dunedin. Even apart from enjoying her company, which we certainly did, she was just the character we needed. But there was a snag, as there so often is. This was Saturday night, and there was to be some Arts Council meeting beginning on Monday morning in Wellington. Early tomorrow evening she would have to fly from Dunedin to Wellington. And tomorrow, we remembered with dismay, was Sunday, the least promising day of the week for visitors in search of experience. We accepted her offer to call for us in her car in the morning, but with no great hopes of the day itself. And there we sadly underestimated the energy, resource and enthusiasm of Shona McFarlane. This Sunday in Dunedin wasn't simply a good day. It still lives in my memory as the peak day of all our days in New Zealand.

It began in good time and quietly, just as it ought to have done. Shona – and there can be no Miss McFarlane now – drove us round the vacant Sunday morning streets to give us our first real look at her city. I shall postpone my impressions of it until the end of this chapter, with some help then from the book she gave us, written and illustrated by herself, *Dunedin : Portrait of a City*. She took us next to the house she shares with her mother, a very pleasant maternal type already busy, I think, making sandwiches for a picnic lunch. We went with Shona to the room she uses as a studio, where she showed us some of her work. It was in a variety of styles and ranged from the tentative to the here-goes-hit-or-miss. If I seem to be condescending to her painting, I will add that she draws better than I will ever be able to do in this lifetime. But I ventured privately to prefer my sense of colour and tone to hers. A few people were now 'dropping in', and these included Shona's sister, Mrs Francis, later to be our hostess. I imagine that Dunedin is a 'dropping-in' place, and as I was brought up in another one I have never objected to droppers-in except of course when I am working. I seemed to catch some muttered conspiratorial talk about that picnic, and I wondered what would come of it because often no good is done by such talk, the gods not favouring it.

Hoping to provide me with a paint, Shona took us along the Otago Peninsula, high but moving rather cautiously into the ocean, quite an important feature of the Dunedin scene. Her choice was Sandfly Bay on the south side, but as we descended towards the sea she agreed with me that it was far too windy to paint outdoors. The wind in fact was rapidly breaking the fine weather we had enjoyed for days. It was almost as if we were entering another climate, and before the afternoon was done we might have moved 1,000 miles nearer the Antarctic. Indefatigable and never lacking an idea, Shona moved us across the Peninsula, to the north side high above Grassy Point and Broad Bay, where Larnach's Castle successfully defied the elements and all disasters except those provided by Larnach's own character and temperament. There was now some arrangement – though I never understood how it was arrived at – that Mr Fred O'Neill, an enthusiastic Theatre man, should collect the picnic lunch and bring it to us at the Castle. (I still had misgivings.) Up the ruined drive we passed quite a number of fellow sightseers. Larnach's Castle obviously tempted people to pay it a visit on a fine Sunday – or what when they had set out had been a fine Sunday. Now it was cold and already showery.

For the benefit of readers outside New Zealand, I must say something about Larnach himself. He was an Australian, born in 1833 and arriving in New Zealand in 1867 as chief manager of the Bank of Otago, which brought him to Dunedin. In 1875 he began a successful political career by being elected M.P. for Dunedin. He seems to have been an able banker and financial public servant, though less fortunate in his private commercial investments. He ran into financial trouble in the 1890's, and finally, in 1898, he committed suicide. He was a widower twice, after having two sons and four daughters by his first wife; but his third wife, who had rejoiced in the name of Constance de Bathe Brandon, survived. Local gossip, which I have not found in print and cannot vouch for, alleges that his final self-destructive urge owed something to his discovery that one of his sons was having an affair with the third wife. 'He was deservedly popular,' the N.Z. Encyclopaedia tells us, 'being by nature open-handed and generous,' but I for one would be more ready to honour his memory if he hadn't built a dungeon under his castle, to lock up poachers and estate workers who came home drunk. For what it is worth, my guess is that he was one of those very clever and ambitious financial men who have a silly side, subject to ideas of grandeur and to folly. The fact that he built his 'castle' as early as the 1870's, spending the equivalent of a million pounds of our money, suggests that he suffered from *hubris* and finally paid the fatal price of it.

On a brighter day Larnach's Castle might have looked more impressive, even after so many melancholy years of neglect. Architecturally, it seemed a Scottish Baronial hotch-potch. So far as I could gather – and I didn't gather much; after all I am not writing a guide book – the building consists of two main storeys, a tower block above them, then a single high turret as a look-out point. What chiefly took my fancy, so that I envied the present owner, Mr Barker, this feature, was a glass-enclosed promenade, complete with some fine white-painted ironwork, on the second floor. Expensive materials and the craftsmen who knew what to do with them were recklessly imported from Europe. But when English oak and rich mahogany had to be brought so far, it seems a pity that even more extensive use wasn't made of New Zealand woods, notably the *kauri*. Indeed, I think Larnach's mistake was his failure to be determinedly colonial, his grand *nouveau riche* desire to import the grandest and richest from everywhere, rather like a man planning a meal, with expense no object, consisting of 20 lbs of caviare, 100 tins of Strasburg *pâté de foie gras*, scores and scores of plovers' and gulls' eggs, and so forth. I admit I did no keen exploring and sightseeing, never reaching the bedrooms, but I did take a peep into 'the withdrawing room', which had some splendid carving, now under glass; and into what has been left of Larnach's Library; and I even went down to the big ballroom (I was in fact looking for a lavatory) that had a special floor not improved, since Larnach's time, by being used as a shelter for sheep during hard winters. This was in the Castle's leanest years, when the magnificent greenhouse, filled with vines, was turned into a hen-house and the vines cut down because the fowls weren't getting sufficient sunlight. I realize that I am not doing justice to Larnach's grandiose creation, but the truth is, that after having some talk with Mr and Mrs Barker, who gallantly acquired the place and are now trying to bring some order into it, I admired them more than I did the Castle itself.

Mr Barker is a youngish bearded Englishman, his wife a slender New Zealand girl. They are a brave pair, braver I would say than Larnach himself ever was. I know nothing about their finances, though they were making something out of sightseers' entrance fees, but the difficulties and hazards they had faced – and were still facing – were obviously formidable. And when I was there they were still not being given any official help. Born and brought up in the West Riding of Yorkshire I could never have followed their example, but even so I could understand their half-admirable, half-daft impulse to acquire and try to run the monster show-place. What I couldn't understand is why the local authorities hadn't taken it over themselves, long before it began drifting towards ruin. I was still wondering about this when I was helping, in what was still left of the great garden, to place chairs round a table, where we could eat our picnic lunch when it arrived. Jacquetta was being enthusiastic about the neighbouring gazebo, really a glass dome, originally lighting some ship's saloon. But no sooner had we arranged the table than several things happened at once. The sun went out; the rain brought sleet with it; Fred O'Neill arrived and parked his car at an eccentric angle; Shona, Jacquetta and I dived into his car, to eat our lunch in it; we discovered that through that malice of the gods most of the food somehow had been left behind. But Fred's news more than made up for this loss. He knew we would want to visit the albatross nesting-ground at Taiaroa Head, a unique colony of these almost fabulous birds that is closed to the public. He had done some urgent tele-phoning, with the result that Mr and Mrs Alan Wright had been given permission to take us behind the severe fencing and to give us a close-up of these astonishing creatures. Hurray!

As we were driven along the Peninsula towards its last high point,

Taiaroa Head (the whole area now a Wild Life sanctuary), the wind lashed the sleet at our windows. It was as if we were somewhere else, a long way from our calm, warm New Zealand days. Once we were out of the car, to climb up to the Albatross Colony, conditions were worse still: we were now in albatross weather, an iced version of the Roaring Forties. We could have done with fur coats; as it was we hadn't even mackintoshes, and the only chattering we did was with our teeth. But the warden and his wife, kindness itself, did their best for us, and there was even some coat swapping. I drew a knee-length thick yellow oilskin that had large flaps for its collar, and these flaps, with the wind driving almost horizontally, rose and banged against my face so that there were moments when I couldn't see, especially on the way back down the hill. However, I was able to have a good view of the birds, and this we owed, the warden told us, to the wild weather, which brought them nearer to practise taking-off, swooping, gliding. This was their only mainland nesting-ground, the others being little islands in remote storm-tossed seas.

What we were seeing were, so to speak, teenage specimens of Royal Albatrosses, the largest of all, the emperors of the petrel line. The albatross that Coleridge's Ancient Mariner so fatally shot with his crossbow must surely have been one of these Royals, but if it was hung round his neck, as Coleridge tells us, the wretched man would have been hardly able to move, for these birds stand 3 to 4 feet tall, weigh about 25 lbs and have a wing span of 12 feet, sometimes even more. Once they leave the nesting ground they fly on and on, between here and Cape Horn and further still, following ships for refuse or feeding greedily on squids, molluscs, and anything edible, resting – even sleeping – on a favourable wind or on the sea itself. Their breeding is a formidable task: they lay a single, large egg every two years, never replacing it if it is destroyed; and it may take a chick three strenuous days to get out of its shell, not leaving the nest until it can feed itself. Then at last off the young birds go, flying on and on over the wildest seas in the world.

R. M. Lockley, in that splendid book he gave me, *Man Against Nature*, describes how he visited this nesting ground and enjoyed an experience even better than ours, which he well deserved to enjoy, being an ornithologist. But then the season was different and the warden was able to take him right up to the birds:

> We walked very slowly right up to where the handsome black and white birds were incubating a single white egg each, in shallow nests on a gentle slope. He sat down alongside one bird, and presently stroked its satin-white head, and with a gentle pressure of his hand invited it to raise its body to reveal the egg. The albatross made no attempt to bite or resist, and afterwards sat complacently to brood once more. I noticed the ring on its leg.
>
> 'You see,' Sam said calmly, 'I know this chap pretty well, and he knows I'm his good friend. He's about thirty years old, according to his ring number; but in any case I know him by his manners and face – as any shepherd knows each sheep in his own flock. Of course he's been away last year, on his biennial holiday, and I won't see him next year. But next year it'll be the turn of the others to come back to Taiaroa; I'm expecting up to nine nesting pairs next year if all those which bred last year return, and maybe one or two young ladies who will be old enough to breed for the first time as well.'

We never got as close to a bird as that. But we did have a fine near-view of our albatrosses, fully-grown but not yet mature, enjoying wind and weather like lads at play, sometimes grouped together, sometimes taking-off, playing with the wind and then returning, with – as Jacquetta noted – 'their huge pink feet pressed out behind them before they settled'. There are moments and scenes that seem to take on a mythological quality, as if we were switched back to a magical age: as when we were staying in Alice Springs and visited a station some miles out, and not far from it we saw a line of big golden kangaroos come bounding out of a wood. There was at least a touch of this, illuminating what was anyhow a rich and memorable experience, in the time we spent that Sunday afternoon out at the nesting-ground – the startling explosion of icy lashing weather; Taiaroa Head itself, looking like the end of the earth; the beautiful great birds with their snowy and ebony plumage and their incredibly long narrow wings, which would soon

take them gliding and swooping and soaring in an air and above seas
we would never know, utterly strange. And as I walked back down the
slope, inspite of the cold and the wind and those yellow oilskin flaps
that kept buffeting and blinding me, I still moved half in a dream.

We were driven then, not too fast at first because our road twisted
and turned along the shore of Otago Harbour, back to the city and
straight to the house of Shona's clever sister, Mrs Francis, a painter.
There she was, with her three daughters, who, I was told, all studied
J.B.P. at their private school, and Laurie, her husband, a genial
lawyer (they do exist) and just the man to be host at a party. For that is
what we found there, good company and food and drink, a party in
full swing and perhaps in even fuller swing when the English guests
arrived. Feeling expansive, perhaps appearing part-stoned, not from
booze but from the albatross encounter, I chatted or rumbled along,
I remember, with some congenial fellow guests. Among these I recall
Gordon Buchanan, literary editor of the *Otago Daily Times*, New
Zealand's first daily paper; Graham Billing, a writer who had been
awarded the Burns Fellowship at the university and his wife, Diana,
who was to interview me later for her weekly, *The Listener*; Professor
and Mrs Sawyer, with whom we dined on Tuesday evening; the
Gerard Currans representing the N.Z.B.C. talks department; Mrs
Hannan, President of the Dunedin Repertory Society, her husband
Jack (backstage expert) and young daughter Debbie, already a
reporter. There were of course a great many others, and, like those
already named, they represented a good cross-section of Dunedin
intelligentsia. There was just one piece of bad luck. We had to say
goodbye to Shona, who had to dash off – and 'dash' is the right word –
to catch her plane to Wellington, where her Arts Council meetings
were unexpectedly protracted for the next few days, so that – alas –
we never saw her again and couldn't express our thanks face-to-face,
only later on paper.

But the party, like the good party it was, continued after Shona had
fled. It astounded me. To have improvised a party of this kind at such
short notice – and on a Sunday too – seemed to me an astonishing feat.
Though we know a lot of people in and around Alveston and Stratford,

and lots more in and around London, we could no more have created a party like this within a few hours than we could fly with the albatrosses. The secret, I suppose, apart from the drive and enthusiasm of Heather and Laurie Francis and Shona herself, is that Dunedin is just the right size, where everybody in artistic and academic circles can rapidly communicate with everybody else. Nevertheless, I have known places this size where you would need a press-gang to stage a party at short notice. Perhaps there is something in the air of Dunedin. However, I will risk another point that will astonish some readers. Much credit must be given to the Scots' background and tradition. But isn't Scotland notorious for mean penny-pinching and every form of stinginess? Yes – and so is Yorkshire. And, my astonished friends, for the same reason. The Scots and the Tykes can afford to have these mean and stingy jokes against them; indeed they often invent these legends themselves; simply because anybody who has lived among them knows they are hospitable and generous. Surrey, let us say, or Herefordshire or Leicester would instantly take offence at such gibes – they might, as people say, be too 'near the knuckle' – so nobody risks them. We Tykes and Scots just laugh – and pass the bottle. And there must be some Yorkshire blood, as well as a lot of Scots blood, in Dunedin.

Monday began well and continued to be favourably disposed towards me until a late hour, when it ended rather badly. Sunday's albatross weather must have gone roaring away during the night; this morning was fairly calm and the sun had come back to us; so we ordered a car to return us to the scene of Sunday's defeat, the view of Sandfly Bay. Though not excited by the sketch I did, looking down on the bay, I felt reasonably satisfied, at least feeling I hadn't wasted a fine morning. A scribble in my little pocket diary – and I wish there were more of them – tells me how I spent the afternoon – *2.30 TV int. 3.50 radio*. And here I think I ought to offer an apology. All these interviews were conducted in an easy friendly fashion – with no 'loaded' questions, as I have already pointed out – but they have all vanished from my memory, partly because there was never any fuss. (I consider myself a cool old hand in the mass media department. After all I was on radio in the 1920's and on TV, strange as it may seem, as early as the 1930's. So I don't bring any fuss with me into the studio.) Moreover, I never saw or heard any of these interviews when they went out on the air. I have a rule against watching and listening to myself performing. It is a sensible rule. If I thought I was bad I would feel depressed, perhaps decide against going on the air again. If I enjoyed my performance, then I would be even more conceited than I am already. What is more important is that I might soon become self-conscious, then fuss would set in, and it is the absence of this, the ability to take the job in my stride and not worry about it, that has made me an occasional welcome performer, at least in the studios if not in the eyes and ears of the public. I always feel that too many people on TV are too anxious to create a favourable impression, smirking at the viewers as if they wanted to borrow money from them. That is why the very old, much older than I am, are often so wonderful on TV: they might die any night and so they don't care a damn what the viewers think about them. Anybody who ever saw on TV – for example – Gordon Craig, Casals, Wanda Landowska the harpsi-chordist – will rush to agree with me. They make the average 'TV personality' look like a used-car salesman.

We had already received at the hotel a note that ran as follows:

> Angus Ross, professor of History, and his wife Margot will pick you up at the Southern Cross Hotel at 7.30 p.m. this evening.
> The other people who will be coming to dinner are:
> Douglas Coombs, Professor of Geology, and his wife Anne;
> Charles Higham, Professor of Anthropology, and his wife Pauline;
> Margaret Dalziel, Professor of English.

This extremely sensible note, which other hosts might copy with advantage, came from R. O. H. Irvine, Vice-Chancellor. I knew that Dr Irvine had been made Vice-Chancellor of Otago University only the day before, which probably meant that the burdens of high office were already heavy on his shoulders, and we thought it uncommonly civil and hospitable of him to add a dinner party to this load. We took at once both to him and to his very attractive wife – a real doctor herself and of a sort unhappily I never find myself consulting. With a cleverly chosen guest list, it was a good dinner party and I left it rather early with much reluctance. (Of that, more later.) Mr right-hand neighbour at the dinner table was Dean Dalziel from Eng. Lit., an amusing and robust talker quite content we should ignore her subject and department. Just once I was trifle sharp with her, though not I hope scowling, grunting or snarling. So far as I cut her short, I did it for her own sake, as we shall see. She had launched, not without a glimmer of humour, into an account of all the advantages enjoyed by anybody living in New Zealand. (And here I had no quarrel with her, as this book should prove.) But when she went on to describe how secure she and her friends would be when we poor devils (my words) in the Northern Hemisphere might be facing starvation, the ultimate pollution, doomsday rain of atomic bombs, I felt she was beginning to take the path where *hubris* and then Nemesis lie in wait. 'You know,' I said, no grunting, no snarling, 'if you go on talking and thinking like that, one morning half the country may blow up in your face.' I knew of course that New Zealand could be in no such danger; but I am genuinely afraid of complacent hubristic talking and thinking, which set the demigods of malice and ironical conclusions to work, something I had noticed, with myself as one of the victims too, time after time. But it remained a dinner party I was very reluctant to leave.

To jump a day but keep to the subject of academic dinner parties, we had another one on Tuesday night, when Professor and Mrs Sawyer entertained us. (We had met them at the Francis's Sunday party.) Jacquetta's brief note – and on the whole she is a more severe critic of social occasions than I am – genuinely expresses our thanks: 'Six at dinner, including the amusing, provocative Professor Taylor, a philosopher. *Jolly*.' And here a general point would not be out of place. We had been hospitably and, to my mind, successfully entertained by academics twice at Wellington, once at Massey, and twice at Dunedin. Now dons can be delightful people, as many I have known have been. They can also be anything but delightful people, being dry, narrow, pedantic, envious, conceited, arrogant; and I have met, though more in print than in person, these types too. They tend to become what Philip Guedalla used to call 'the stealthy assassins' who lurk, knife in hand, in the anonymous columns of *The Times Literary Supplement*. Do such academics exist in New Zealand? Possibly they do but are carefully omitted from guest lists when visitors are to be entertained. But it is a fact that on the five occasions mentioned above I never even caught a glimpse of one of their sour faces. I can say nothing about the academics of Christchurch and Auckland because either by chance or design (theirs, not mine) I never met a single one of them. But certainly all those I did meet elsewhere proved to be good company.

However, now I must explain why I had to leave Dr Irvine's very pleasant dinner party on the Monday night. Through urgent messages and an actual call at the hotel, I had been pressed – one might almost say 'pressurized' – to pay a visit to an amateur Little Theatre group. Late in the evening would do. Finally I agreed to go because I felt that so far in New Zealand I hadn't been in contact with the Theatre at all, either amateur or professional, and this was hardly good enough for a visiting dramatist. Having accepted the engagement, I did what I imagine most people do, I treated myself to a picture of what would happen. I saw myself meeting a small group of enthusiasts and then asking or answering questions, giving them, if they wanted it, the benefit of my years of theatrical experience, which was extensive and not limited to the writing of plays. And I was quite wrong.

Nothing of the sort had been planned. True, I was shown – and asked to admire – the stage and the tiny 80-seat auditorium that had been ingeniously contrived out of what had been part of a private house. But instead of a serious small group, wanting to ask and to answer equally serious questions, what I found was a large noisy party, apparently consisting of people no more interested in me and the present and future of the Theatre than I was in the statistics of the timber trade. People don't have to be interested in me and my opinions – there are times when I lose interest in these myself – but I didn't see why I should have been put under pressure, then compelled to forsake an agreeable dinner party, just to catch this babble of self-important performers and a few superior patrons of this minikin 'experimental Theatre'. Let anybody put this down to wounded vanity if he or she pleases, but this almost press-ganged engagement seemed to me a dead loss, the only one I remember out of our whole visit.

Moreover, I felt there was an atmosphere created by these people that was unfavourable to the kind of Theatre in which I believed. I had already learnt from our new friend Fred O'Neill that he was up to his neck, spending all day and half the night, raising a fund to buy Dunedin's old Regent Theatre, a real playhouse capable of seating a reasonably adequate audience and of supporting, I trust, a highly professional repertory company. (Sooner or later it could exchange visits with similar companies in the other cities.) The contemporary Theatre may need verse and experiment, Brecht's communist propaganda, the antics of Ionesco, the deepening gloom and brevity of Beckett, the theatre of Cruelty or the Absurd, and all the rest of it; but what is needed first of all is hard-working disciplined professionalism and the presence in the audience of plenty of ordinary people, as distinct from self-conscious aesthetes. The Theatre worth working for and fighting for is the Theatre that can be taken into and enjoyed by the community. And that, I imagine, is what a Dunedin enthusiast like Fred O'Neill has in mind throughout all his fund-raising – to acquire for the city not another adapted drawing-room but a genuine playhouse like the Regent. Good luck to him!

It must have been on the bright Tuesday morning, I think, that I took a stroll round the streets near the hotel, before we set out in a hired car to find a good painting place outside the city. After half an hour I had to give it up – and for a curious reason. The night before I must have been seen on TV, because every fifty yards or so somebody stopped me, told me who I was, and insisted on shaking hands warmly. This was gratifying, and testified to the friendliness of the city, but soon became embarrassing – no doubt I am vain but I am no exhibitionist – so that I retreated to the Southern Cross. Ignoring Otago Peninsula this time we drove along the high road above the

north shore of Otago Harbour, finally descending to look at Port
Chalmers and Carey's Bay and Deborah, all worth looking at but not
offering me what I wanted, even though I couldn't have said exactly
what I did want. After much to-ing and fro-ing, with the morning and
everybody's patience wearing away, I found something I wanted to
paint, though even with a large-scale map in front of me here I can't
give it a name. It was a stretch of water enclosed by coloured cliffs and
with a hint of sandbanks towards the foreground. I am nearly always
at my worst when I take a lot of trouble, probably because I don't
really know what trouble to take, and am either at my best or quite
hopeless when circumstances compel me to work fast, as hard as I can
go. This was one of the fast jobs, hell-for-leather and forget-the-
detail, that didn't seem hopeless – a quick, jaunty, cheeky sketch – so
that at almost the last moment I was well satisfied with my morning.

After lunch Jacquetta went round the Early Settlers' Museum
with its curator, Mr Homan, noting with approval the way in which
its walls were covered with innumerable Early Settler portrait
photographs and paintings, the excellent collection of settlers'
furniture, china, costumes, and – the Museum's pride and joy – the
facing-both-ways engine. I think it was at this time that I was breaking
my rule against giving any more press interviews, the point being that
now TV and radio had taken their place. But a young man with a
marked Scots accent rang me up from the local paper, asking for an
interview, and when I said 'No', he told me he had only recently
arrived in the country. I had in fact been longer in New Zealand and
had seen far more of it. This then, if I agreed, would be new-comer
interviewed by a newer-comer; therefore, too good to miss. So
instead of joining Jacquetta among the Early Settlers, I talked in our
sitting-room with the Latest Settler, who turned out to be a shortish,
perky, eager chap, as ready to be interviewed as to interview.

He had been working quite well on a Glasgow paper when he
suddenly decided he wanted to go to New Zealand. Apparently there
were openings here for newspapermen: he was accepted at once as an
immigrant. He also found a job at once on a Dunedin paper. To my
surprise, he admitted that he was being paid less than the Glasgow

paper had been paying him, but didn't feel as strongly as I did that New Zealand is a fairly expensive country. (This difference is easily explained. I was reckoning costs in terms of either sterling or American dollars whereas in terms of the exchange then current, the N.Z. Dollar outranked both of them.) His smaller salary didn't seem to worry him; but then I think he was confident that promotion would soon come his way, being an eager and ambitious young Scot, just right for Dunedin. One thing he said, quite sincerely, offered me considerable relief. It was always possible that moving around as I did, on a semi-de-luxe celebrity jaunt, I might have been deceiving myself – and all my readers – when I found these Kiwis all so open and friendly. But how would a young newspaperman, straight out of the egg here and living on a reduced salary, find them? Well, he had found people open and friendly too. So then I allowed him to interview me, to give him something to take back to his paper. But what he wrote I never saw. For all I know he may have found me far from open and friendly, perhaps insufferable.

There is some confusion about that Tuesday afternoon. Perhaps I saw the young Scot not at the beginning but at the end of the afternoon, because Jacquetta says in her notes that Mr Homan of the Early Settlers drove her to join me in the Art Gallery. And certainly I remember going to the Art Gallery, now (since 1925) in a park, which is perhaps where an art gallery ought to be. Its curator or director, Mr Lloyd, took me, then us, around its well-lighted walls. He seemed to me a courteous and sensible man, and this is higher praise than it may first appear to be, for while most men in charge of art galleries are courteous, not all of them are sensible. This Dunedin collection offers no astounding masterpieces but very little rubbish; it appeared to be strongest in eighteenth-century portraits (including some Gainsboroughs) and early English watercolours; rather weak in later nineteenth-century work, though I noticed a good Tissot; and the best-known Dunedin artist, Frances Hodgkins, had two rooms to herself. Though she returned to New Zealand for short periods, she spent most of her life in England; and I can't help wondering if her art wouldn't have gained by being nourished longer by her roots.

Towards the end of her life and just after her death in 1947 her later work, chiefly very personal *gouaches*, came into vogue – there was almost a cult of her – and I remember acquiring several of her paintings myself. But it is possible to admire work at first and then discover you no longer want to live with it, perhaps because you have not chosen well and not because you dismiss the artist. Certainly there was work of hers in these two Dunedin Gallery rooms I would be proud to own. Also on display were awards in the Banks' Competition, in which we were glad to see that our new friend, Mrs Francis, had taken a 2nd Prize. And if our far wealthier banks in London organize and finance artistic competitions of this kind, then I have never been around when their awards have been announced and on show.

If I did all this on Tuesday, then what was I doing on Wednesday morning, our last in Dunedin? I know what that indefatigable searcher into the past, Jacquetta, was doing: 'I went to the Hocken Library where I was met by the director, Mr Hitchings, and was taken by him to the Art Department. Looked at the early water-colours, a quite distinctive group of Dunedin painters. I went through to the Museum and spent another hour with Stuart Park. He believes that the Maori culture could have been, and probably was, a matter of internal development from the earliest Polynesian inhabitants of about 800 A.D. He warned me that Mr Duff of Christchurch (author of *The Moa Hunters*) would strongly disagree.' So much for busy and conscientious Jacquetta. But what was Idle Jack doing? My guess, for I haven't a single note, is that I divided the morning between packing and then taking a last look round the centre of the city. If you who read this should ever be invited to go on a journey with me, don't hesitate to refuse at once. I am a bad traveller, showing no sign of improvement after going so far so often. I am fussy and apprehensive – yes, apprehensive because I am fussy, and fussy because I am apprehensive. In this matter I am always at odds with my otherwise delightful wife. She likes to arrive just in time for the plane or the train, whereas I always want to be early at the airport or the railway station. In the same fussy, apprehensive style, I do most of my

packing hours before anybody is ready to handle my luggage. I must
have some deep-seated fear of all travel, though my anxiety dreams
are never about planes crashing or trains going off the line but about
finding myself nearly at plane or train time and then realizing that my
baggage is miles away in the wrong direction; but the fear is there, so
that always when I begin to pack, no matter what the temperature of
the room is, I start to sweat. So probably I left the hotel to cool off as
well as to take a last look at Dunedin.

It is an odd city, though I hasten to add that it is perhaps my first
choice among the four cities we came to know, however superficially.
There was a time when I used to say that if I were kicked out of
England, refusing at last to beggar myself trying to pay super-tax, I
would go at once to British Columbia and live just outside Vancouver.
Now I think it would be Dunedin. But does that make it odd? Not at
all: Dunedin is odd entirely by itself. For example, it has the largest
area of all the major cities and yet it has the smallest population. Again,
though its population is only about 85,000, somehow it always gave
me the impression that it had three times that number of citizens, not
an idea that any English town of 85,000 would ever suggest. It was a
certain grand civic style that made me want to treble its population.
But while I was actually there I never fully appreciated its fine
buildings, with their massive or decorative fronts, their towers and
spires. To do that in a short time, while moving around on other
errands, a man needs a quick architectural eye, which I haven't got
and never pretend to have. To tell the truth, in this particular respect
I have enjoyed and appreciated Dunedin far more sitting here at home,
going at my leisure through Shona McFarlane's *Portrait of a City*,
guided and stimulated by her pencil and brush and affectionate
jottings. But here again oddness creeps in, for Shona's portrait, good
as it is, has to be corrected by the general impression the city makes on
a visitor; and while I am not an architectural man I am a fairly good
general impression man. And I couldn't help feeling that what had
been once a noble attempt to create a South Pacific Edinburgh, with
the best of it still there, had been leased more recently to Ohio and
Southern California. The result isn't hopeless but it *is* rather con-

fused and messy. Furthermore – and I add this without knowing Dunedin's domestic history – I was troubled by a vague feeling that the city must have been governed alternatively by wise men and blockheads.

Even so, I would gladly return there. I could find stout reasons for this. To begin with, its surroundings are magnificent, though in this respect it isn't unique among New Zealand cities. But the long Otago Peninsula, with its treasury of preserved wild life (of which the albatrosses are only a part) and its suggestion of strange wild seas, is certainly unique. I would enjoy too the presence of a ring of virgin bush, like a more romantic 'green belt' in England, and the absence of sprawling suburbs so that you seem to enter the city immediately and dramatically. Shona McFarlane, in her Introduction, boldly declares that 'Dunedin has great charm'. I won't venture to say that it hasn't – after all she knows and I am only popping in and out and then guessing – but I must add that to my mind it isn't Dunedin but Christchurch that I associate with charm, which it probably acquired, so to speak, on lend-lease from the Anglican Church. Dunedin, the old Scots citadel so far from Edinburgh and Inverness, has something else that seems to me more important than charm. It has a tradition, it has a spirit, it has an atmosphere, of which the Octagon with its statue of Burns, the fine churches, the University's splendid original building, are the visible symbols. The bracing air of the place helps to sustain life and breed character. The fact that it has concentrated itself, not sprawling over and ruining its countryside, is all in its favour. In this respect it has an essentially New Zealand character, for like New Zealand it has kept itself reasonably small and has not gone out of its mind, crazily developing itself for more money and power, more prestige and more misery.

Yet during the few days I was there, although I enjoyed those days, I couldn't bring myself to believe that Dunedin had fulfilled its magnificent early promise, all the dreams that must have inspired its immigrant elders. Though Shona McFarlane and her friends had achieved an Arts Council, and by the time this book is in the shops they may have acquired the Regent Theatre, I did get the impression

when I was there that such wholesome enthusiasts were having to
deal with a dead weight of apathy, were trying to swim towards their
goals across a lake of thick mud and treacle. Here, guessing again, I
may be wrong. But what is surely a fact and not a guess is that this city,
whose tradition, spirit, atmosphere I was so eager to admire, offered
us a cultural scene that in its turn, apart from the museums and the
University, had very little indeed to offer us. The potential was there
but somehow had not been realized. And this, I felt, had nothing to do
with size and wealth. Anything on the grand scale of Christchurch's
new Town Hall and Arts Centre might not be possible, but the vision
the desire, the effort, ought to be possible, especially with such
traditions and all that bracing air. This is a city that ought to take off
like one of its albatrosses.

But I refuse to say *Goodbye* to Dunedin – and it must be *Goodbye*
and not *Au revoir*, alas! – in a negative critical spirit. What it had to
offer it gave generously, on all sides, and the gift was precious because
it consisted of an instant warm friendliness. (Anybody who imagines
this to be common form everywhere mustn't travel as often and as far
as I have done, but stay at home.) Of the four major New Zealand
cities we stayed in, Dunedin has stayed in my mind, a smiling image,
as the friendliest. I have no golden award to make, but here at least
from one visiting Englishman is a feather to stick in its cap – or
bonnet.

Now we had to go. Derek's itinerary told us firmly; *Depart Dunedin
3.40 p.m. by NAC 464*. Besides, we had already exchanged letters with
Dame Ngaio Marsh, an old friend who had stayed with us in England,
and we knew that she had arranged a grand dinner party for us that
night in Christchurch, to which Derek's *NAC 464* would fly us. Fred
O'Neill, taking an afternoon off from saving the Regent, had kindly
insisted upon driving us to the airport. Even I, the old fussy apprehensive traveller, felt comparatively at ease for once. We were in good
time; our places on the plane had been secured; we were due in
Christchurch at 4.25 – a nice little flight. But I ought to have known
better than to feel so complacent. Clearly there was something wrong
with this airport: no cars and no people outside; no baggage and no

people inside; it was like an airport in some uneasy dream. At last we found one man still on duty. He was in fact a nice fellow, but in his voice there was that inevitable ironic cheerfulness, that almost triumphant tone, when he told us that, owing to the strike, there would be no plane to Christchurch that day. 'And I wouldn't say you'd get on to one tomorrow,' he added, not quite smiling. Unprintable epithets ran through my head but didn't reach my mouth, though it was wide open, not in wonder but despair.

CHAPTER 9

At Christchurch

What followed at the airport deserves to be explored a little. After the man had taken our tickets for the cancelled flight and was then giving me the money the airline owed, he said casually, 'You might charter a plane from the Aero Club to take you to Christchurch.' Kindly note that *casually*. I find in it the essence of New Zealand life and character. Down there they are going to be as casual as they can. But what about us, not a plane-chartering pair? Here to fly away and hating to disappoint Ngaio, Jacquetta lit up at this suggestion. I asked a question or two, found that the cost would not be wildly unreasonable, and agreed that the pilot of the little plane, up and around somewhere, should be called down from the sky. Though I shared my wife's feelings about the wretched present situation, I doubt if I did any lighting up. The prospect of flying as far as Christchurch in a tiny light plane was more than daunting, almost terrifying. I am not exactly a coward – and indeed Jacquetta fondly believes I am a brave man – but as we have already seen I am naturally apprehensive. I am a heavy and rather bulky man, needing plenty of support and space high in the air, and I am horrified when asked to entrust myself to a flying machine apparently put together out of four deck-chairs. So many a gloomy thought darkened my mind during the twenty minutes we waited for the pilot. He proved to be a large amiable young man, very casual indeed, but his plane seemed even smaller than I had imagined it would be – a kind of three deck-chair job. There was just room for me to wedge myself in beside the pilot and for Jacquetta to share the seat behind – God knows how; I never knew – with all our luggage. So off we went, with apprehension at first drying up my mouth so that I could barely ask a question – and a casual question at that.

We ascended into a wonderful surprise. Out of all the innumerable flights I must have made – some of them just after World War II, flying around Central Europe, the Soviet Union, Scandinavia, very rough – this was easily the best flight I had ever known. The big jets, particularly the Jumbos, boast about their smooth rides, but they are rough-and ready switchbacks compared to this little marvel of a plane. It is no exaggeration to declare that this was the only occasion in which I *really enjoyed flying itself*, as so many born pilots must have done. Absolutely steady at 5,000 feet, without bumps, twists, rises and falls, we made straight for Christchurch like a giant bee. The late afternoon was calm, sunny, clear, and it was a delicious pleasure to be aloft in it. All unease having vanished, we could look down and enjoy all that passed below: the bare lower slopes of what I took to be the Kakanui Mountains; the crawling and faintly foaming sea of the Canterbury Bight; and then the intense cultivated sections of the Canterbury Plain that looked from the air like variegated squares of polished wood. Not a dull moment. But there was little time for talk with the pilot because – rather to my astonishment – he was so busy exchanging information with airports behind and ahead of us, just as if we were a Jumbo jet carrying three hundred passengers. (This isn't a sneer; he was being conscientious, though perhaps he might have been taking a certain pleasure in overdoing it a bit.) He took us down as quietly and efficiently as he had taken us up. We alighted in triumph in our unfamiliar role as plane-charterers. Jacquetta never swaggers, but I tend to do at times, and no doubt I did then. (In the days when I often played tennis at Queen's Club, I was partnering an old tennis-hand, almost a pro, and when I re-joined her, after doing something swift and decisive at the net, she said, 'When you've played a good shot, try not to show it.' That was over 40 years ago and I no longer play tennis, but perhaps I still 'show it'.) This airport was nearly as quiet as the one we had left, but somehow a photographer was there and insisted upon our posing for him. I never saw that photograph – did we gleam or glitter with triumph or did we try to suggest blasé charterers' boredom? – but if that photographer or anybody else happens to have a copy to spare, I would be much obliged if I could take a look at it. We thanked our pilot warmly and he acknowledged our thanks with a nice little gesture on his part. Because he would have to stay overnight in Christchurch, I had agreed to add to the cost of the flight something for his board and lodging. But he returned half of it, saying that what he kept would be ample. This may happen everywhere, but I would be ready to bet that it happens oftener in New Zealand.

We were lucky enough to find a taxi outside the airport. We were also lucky in where he took us, but this needs some explanation. We had asked Derek to book us into a comparatively old-fashioned hotel in the city, and we weren't pleased when he let us know that this hotel being full he had had to send us to a certain new Avon Motor Lodge. So were we out of luck? We were not for soon we discovered we couldn't have done better. True, we had no view, but after all I had been enjoying plenty of views, and here we had a quiet and commodious suite. Our first sight of the sitting room set us gaping. It seemed to be full of flowers and fruit. We might have been greeted elsewhere with a few blooms or two or three apples. But Christchurch could be about to hold a harvest festival for us. All this coming on top of our plane-charterers' triumph set me swaggering around that suite like a minor politician or a film-star of the second rank. And not for the first time, I swaggered too soon. While I enjoyed Christchurch, with a few exceptions to be noted later Christchurch showed no desire to enjoy me. Not many eager invitations came our way. When I recorded a TV interview, the boys in the studio almost yawned in my face so that I began to wonder what I was doing there. Don't misunderstand me; I haven't to be made a fuss of; I can take what has been described to me since as 'aristocratic reserve'. However, the genuine aristocrats I have known have had less reserve than bourgeois types like myself. Most of them have had loud voices, casual manners and a very sharp eye for the main chance.

Gerald Lascelles, barrister and bachelor, came promptly to take us to Dame Ngaio's house. His passion is for music, which we discussed in the car, and it was only afterwards that I learnt that Dame Ngaio roped him into her Shakespeare productions, to play, I was told, 'Falstaffs and Pistols', rather as if there were dozens of them. (Incidentally, during the evening, our hostess, eyeing me wistfully, told me I would make a 'perfect Falstaff'. I am still wondering if she said that because she thought I wouldn't need much padding, or because she felt I had the voice for the part – which I have – or realized I was not without wit myself. I must ask her sometime what she had in her mind at that moment.) Dame Ngaio's house emerged through the foliage on top of an unexpected steep little hill. She has a delightful and rather small old family house. That *old* is worth discussing. I cannot speak for other people, but over and over again I have found myself unconsciously adopting the standards of the place I am in, so genuinely gaping in wonder and admiration at what is considered old there, clean forgetting that I owned and occupied houses far older at home. So, for example, when I first visited New Orleans and was taken round the French Quarter there, wonder-struck at the age of its houses – quaint old wicked haunts – quite forgetting that I owned and lived in a Georgian house in London and a seventeenth-century manor house (haunted too) in the Isle of Wight. In the same way I made no comparisons when I entered Dame Ngaio's house; I looked at it, we might say, through New Zealand eyes; and what I saw was a remarkably *old* house. And a charming one.

It was altogether an exceptionally good dinner party. Our hostess had brought to it her considerable social experience and her drama director's eye for décor and detail. We tried to match the excellent food and wine with our talk, sitting at a round table in a panelled dining-room, looking across the flames from the great silver candelabra. It was almost like the first act of a high comedy at the Josefstadt, Vienna. We were a mixed but civilized lot, with some ballast of legal folk and academics but with the Theatre never far away. So David Hindin might be running the family business but he looked like a handsome Shakespearean leading man – and that is exactly what he is when Dame Ngaio is directing. A late-comer, Mervyn Thompson, from the Eng. Lit. department at the university, was obviously destined to make his mark directing plays. He and I talked Theatre. (It is so easy to begin talking Theatre and so hard to leave off.) But one of that night's new acquaintances we soon regarded as a friend: Mrs Helen Holmes.

Helen and her late husband, Lyall, a brilliant construction engineer whose comparatively early death was a cruel disaster, were among my eldest daughter's friends. Not too easy to please, she admired them both, Helen especially after she had lost Lyall and had to begin life all over again as a widow with a family of young children. What she had to face, through accidents and illnesses, need not be mentioned here, but what must be mentioned is her courage and gallant attractive bearing, a fortitude more often displayed by women, I believe, than by men. Helen and Lyall were two of Ngaio's first student players; and now after so many years Helen has a deep regard and increasing affection for Christchurch's famous Dame: a fact that speaks well for both ladies. Lyall Holmes played a notable part in the creation of the new Town Hall (and Performing Arts Centre), and when Helen offered to show it to us next morning we were delighted to accept her invitation.

The best short description of this Christchurch Town Hall is that it's a knock-out. We have a number of cities in England that could make Christchurch look like a little town, but not one of these cities – I am excluding London – can show us anything they have built for many years that can match this Town Hall. From now on nobody in Birmingham, Manchester, Liverpool, Leeds, Newcastle, can afford to regard New Zealand as something small, remote, dullish, merely packed with potential lamb chops and butter. The building – or, rather, the complex of buildings – is cunningly sited close to the Avon River, which must feed its impressive fountain. Helen Holmes was able to borrow a fat ring of keys that admitted us everywhere – 'backstage', so to speak, as well as all 'front of house' – so that we saw everything, onward and upward from the immense foyer.

They are right in their brochure to call this a Complex: a restaurant on the ground floor, overlooking the river; bars and promenades on the two Mezzanine Floors; then two big conference and banqueting rooms, large enough to be comfortably divided; finally the elliptical Auditorium and the James Hay Theatre; with the entire colour scheme being based on varying shades of what I can only call Chinese red lacquer. The Auditorium is a superb job. It can cope with an orchestra of 120, a choir of 400, an audience of over 2,300, yet is not forbiddingly unintimate, no monster. After briefly trying out its acoustics, I felt ready to bet a few pounds that they are better than those of the Royal Festival Hall and the Lincoln Center concert hall. It can be used for meetings but I hope there will not be too many of them but plenty of Mozart, Beethoven, Brahms and Wagner, for surely it is these men – and not presidents, chairmen, secretaries, movers of amendments, passers of resolutions – that the planners, designers, builders of this Auditorium had in mind. As for the James Hay Theatre, it is fan-shaped, holds 1,000, and has everything 'back and front' (including civilized dressing-rooms) that so many of us have dreamt about, including, I imagine, our friend Dame Ngaio, who set it going with a Shakespeare production. Here, in a whisper, I must add that I believe the play was Henry V, no favourite of mine, because I wish Shakespeare had killed off Henry and then gone on with Falstaff.

Still glowing and dizzy with enthusiasm – for it really is, I repeat, a knock-out – we were taken by Helen to a pleasant, oldish club. There we were to meet the club's President, who was kindly inviting us to lunch. Probably still dizzy I heard some confused talk about our meeting him, and when a young and innocent waitress – and this description is important – led me away I thought she was taking me to some official quarter of the club, which might include a presidential hide-out. Pointing at a door, the little waitress said, 'It's through there.' Imagining some nest of offices, I said, 'But what do I do when I go through there?' She made no reply, but hurried away. Less than a minute later, I understood why. That door was the entrance to the men's lavatory. But is this little tale worth telling? To my mind it is, for I have lived long enough to appreciate, to enjoy or to fear, the growth and the force of gossip, malicious anecdotes, legends and myths. I must do whatever I can to kill the story of the visiting English author who asked the young waitress at the club what he should do when he reached the men's lavatory. *Get this* – as they say in American detective stories – I had every reason to believe the president's room was behind that door.

It must have been that evening which we spent with the Christchurch Branch of the Dickens Fellowship. It had already contributed flowers or fruit or both to our sitting-room, and had then given me a warm and rather urgent invitation to visit it. I felt too close to being a fraud about this. True, I was down as one of its vice-presidents, and had made a speech at a huge grand dinner at the Guildhall (very Dickensy this) to mark the centenary of Dickens's death. But I was not really a Fellowship man, never attending its meetings or going on its expeditions. Not that I despised it, but I was both too busy and too lazy. If this seems odd, I am sorry, but I think other creative people will know what I mean. I have expended a vast amount of energy on my work – writing fervently about Dickens among other things – but then feel lazy at once when the work is done.

The Fellowship had taken a long room in an hotel, where chairs had been placed all round the walls. After a chat and a drink with the leading members, I was taken round the seated company, to shake hands and say something here and there. They were nearly all very Dickensy people, almost as if they had been left over from some of his novels. No pejorative sense is intended here; none of his villains or obvious idiots was present; they were amiable and sensible people; but so many of them seemed still to exist in a mid-Victorian Dickensian atmosphere, far removed from nuclear bombs, computers, supermarkets, and what I have called *Admass*. After I had gone the rounds there was a silent air of expectancy. They were ready for a long speech, perhaps a solemn address. After I had spoken rather briefly, I sensed disappointment. We were at cross-purposes in this matter of speaking, and this is why I hope that some members of the Christchurch Dickens Fellowship will read this book, because in the next chapter I consider these cross-purposes and the way in which I left so many people in New Zealand feeling disappointed. Meanwhile, I take this opportunity of thanking the Dickens Fellowship for its hospitality, all in the genial spirit of the Master.

By this time we were beginning to take in and appreciate the city itself, with some help from our new driver, Mr Rigby, most obliging and very keen but not free from a desire to pontificate on occasion. The verdant charm of Christchurch reveals itself almost at a first glance. It looks as if it might have been lent to New Zealand by the Anglican Church – at its best. Certainly it began with two pieces of great good luck: it was founded by fairly pious English gents who brought over some reliable workmen; it was built on level ground that encouraged the Avon to meander, while the river in turn inspired the creation of some delightful little bridges. (Some glimpses of the river banks, with canoes and grass lollers well in sight, reminded us not of Oxford, the place of its genesis, but of our own Cambridge 'backs'.) Further acquaintance, however, made me wonder if the Englishness of Christchurch had not been over-emphasized, though this does not mean that anything derogatory is on its way towards this paragraph. Yes, there is the Cathedral, with its shaded grounds. There, so sensibly and often beautifully maintained, are all the trees, the lawns, the gardens. Then again, there is Christ's College, and its Gothic quadrangle, and its straw-hatted, stiff-collared, school-tied pupils, almost like an English public school preserved in gelatine. And finally – though I could go on much longer – there is the local attitude of mind, the psychology of the citizens, said to be steeped in a smugly complacent conservatism, and in this respect not very different from many English cathedral cities. Well then?

But does Christchurch really suggest an English cathedral city? And if so, which one? I can't name it. I am not saying it is better or worse – though if pressed I would say it is better to live in – but that it is different. It represents a dream carried 13,000 miles, down into the Antipodes, and subtly changing as soon as it began to be realized. I am not thinking now, for example, of that huge office block in Cathedral Square, about as nicely placed – to quote my late friend Raymond Chandler – as a scorpion on a plate of angel food. These

monsters can go up anywhere now – curse the luck! No, I am thinking again of those trees, lawns and gardens – but this time not only
those on or near the river but also those found all over the place.
Most of what they offer came originally from England, but it has
suffered a sea-change. The scene is no longer English; not worse,
rather better on the whole. There has been more energy at work here,
even turning the willows by the river into giants. I had read many
references to the sleepiness and lackadaisical air of Christchurch, but
now I no longer believed them. This city, which even now has only
about 170,000 inhabitants, could not have arrived at and maintained
its present appearance, could not have offered its citizens such an
astonishingly wide range of clubs, associations, activities (I stopped
counting them after 300), if most people here had been half-asleep. If
there is any English town in the same *170,000 pop.* bracket that has
achieved as much during this last hundred years, then I have never
been in it. As for that smugly complacent conservatism, then what
about this new Town Hall, bursting above the river like a Chinese-
red-lacquer bomb?

Even if I were about to ramble, I would have a good excuse because
this is a city that asks you to ramble, even if its street plan, deriving
from the early settlement, tends to be rectangular. But I have a point
to make. I found it, one might say, in Christchurch's Canterbury
Museum. Now while Jacquetta, in her thorough professional
fashion, was examining its huge collection of exhibits, objects,
significant artefacts, under the enthusiastic guidance of Mr Duff,
head of the Museum, I spent much of the time lurking downstairs.
The truth is, I was fascinated by that life-size reproduction of a
mid-Victorian Christchurch street. (After all, hadn't I written a
whole book, *Victoria's Heyday*, about the 1850's?) I hung about that
street so long that I believe I wouldn't have been surprised if a
policeman in a strange uniform had arrived to ask me to move along. I
was almost waiting for that cab to find a fare and go clattering off, for
that whiskered man in the toyshop to suggest I bought something,
for that woman in the upstairs window either to give me a smile and
come down or retire in disgust, for the humbler cottage woman to

start cooking on that fire she had: it was as if I had just landed from a short trip in a time-machine. What a splendid idea that street, so carefully reproduced, embodies! What an effect it has on any man, like me, who is time-haunted!

However, I have not yet come to the point I want to make. In 1850 four small ships, filled with the so-called Anglican 'Pilgrims', landed on the neighbouring coast. Where Christchurch is now, there was the river sluggishly moving through a good deal of swampy and inhospitable ground. The original scheme of the Canterbury Association, eagerly discussed in many a senior common room and deanery, was a partial failure. Yet its chief settlement, the future city of Christchurch, was carefully planned, the swamps were drained and building began. And before ten years had gone, there were streets like the one reproduced in the Museum, no rough pioneering shanty-town jobs, but genuine civilized streets, perhaps closer to real civilization than that we have now. I may be naïve, but this seems to me a marvel. First a few little ships and unknown territory; and then, by about the time my father was born, only about 30 years before I was born, a flourishing town, with all manner of plans for ambitious building. What courage, energy, resourcefulness and self-confidence these early settlers had, not only here but elsewhere in New Zealand! (Their piety, Anglican or Free Kirk, played its part here. They didn't feel they were an accident in the universe and on a conveyor-belt to extinction.) If I wonder at New Zealand and it seems to me an extraordinary country, one reason is that so much has been done by a small and scattered population, and another is that it has been all so *recent*, well within the memory of elderly men I knew in my youth. I can't get over it. And there is something else worth remembering – that out of these leafy streets, gardens and shaded lawns of Christchurch there marched, to fight and die in far-distant places, some of the toughest infantry and cavalry of modern times.

On Saturday, our last full day and fortunately bright with clear sunlight, we were given a sight of the magnificent country not too far from Christchurch. This came out of a picnic expedition organized by Ngaio – and why a 'Dame' when we have known her for years? –

and her friend and now ours, Helen Holmes. Helen took her own car and two young daughters, and we followed with Ngaio and Mr Rigby in his car. Moving north-west on the Greymouth Road, we climbed to about 3,000 feet over Porter's Pass and then turned off into a delightful glade, once the site of a homestead belonging to the Enys family. (Mount Enys itself, over 7,000 feet, dominated the neighbourhood.) Before the picnic had to be unpacked, Jacquetta and the two long-legged girls set out for a strenuous walk, with Ngaio and Helen taking a short stroll in the same direction. I had found something to paint, almost straight ahead of me, where two immensely tall yellowing poplars could be seen against a pinkish mountainside, with a variety of foliage, some of it dark fir and beeches nearer the foreground of grass and rusty soil. Ever since I got home I have been meaning to touch up this sketch, with more yellow ochre on those two giant poplars, but either I have been too busy or too lazy.

During our excellent lunch in this little Arcadia, for the first and last time in this country we were plagued by wasps, which must have had a nest round there. I am sure I am right in believing that New Zealand had no native wasps; nobody in his senses would have imported them from England; so by some cunning waspish hocus-pocus they must have arranged their own immigration. They didn't ruin a good picnic but they certainly tried hard. Leaving Helen, Jacquetta and the two girls to potter about, with Ngaio sitting apart and perhaps brooding over the next clever move of her Chief-Inspector Alleyn, Mr Rigby and I went down some side-road where there was a good view of a gorge. And again I did a paint, and some of it is right and some of it just won't do, because somehow I missed suggesting the depth of the gorge, and again I have been meaning to improve it and as yet have done nothing. (Except write this book, give advice about the revival of two or three of my plays, and answer letters and letters and letters and pay bills that are ever-increasingly steep and monstrous.) On the way back I told Ngaio we had arranged to attend an amateur production of *The Winter's Tale* that night, incidentally the only theatrical performance I was able to see during the whole of our visit. Without asperity or any flavour of malice, she said I would probably not enjoy myself, simply because there had recently been several large-scale amateur productions so that the pick of the local talent would not have been available for *The Winter's Tale*.

It wasn't and I didn't. The eye was not displeased – the director, feminine, had in fact some good visual ideas – but the ear and most of the mind were not pleasured. *The Winter's Tale* was an odd choice, unless the director felt that the appearance of sympathetic shepherds would pull in audiences from all over the Canterbury Plain. It is in fact an odd play. I have seen it in London with superb casts, on the highest professional level, and yet, apart from the rustic scenes in Act IV, I have never really enjoyed it. For once Shakespeare cannot make me believe in the character who sets all the action going, Leontes, an impossible fellow from beginning to end, a capering shadow, unworthy of any Hermione. And the whole main plot, based on Greene's novel, is silly. Act IV is of course Shakespeare's own creation, full of wonderful things, and I feel any production stands or falls according to the effect this act has upon us. On Saturday night in Christchurch, it fell and refused to stand, even though some conscientious work had gone into it. But then there was one fault throughout, fatal to a Shakespeare production. Almost all the players' voices lacked body and resonance. Not that they spoke in a Kiwi manner; most traces of the local accent had vanished, rather to my surprise; but nearly all their voices, we might say, were not enjoying themselves, as they should in Shakespeare; it would have been better if they had gone the other way, assuming they were capable of it, giving us more 'ham' and far less refined bread in the sandwich. Clearly this is no general criticism of Christchurch's or the whole country's theatrical activities, but simply an honest impression of the only production I was able to attend. Next time – but alas I must remember there won't be a next time.

I was remembering this when, on Sunday afternoon, we took the plane for Rotorua, for a sight of the thermal region and to keep a date I had with the Booksellers' Conference at Wairakei. I don't know who first called the plane we had to use the *Friendship*, but as far as I was concerned they were far too optimistic. I had made, I trust, many new friends, but this plane was not among them. It was completely full, rather stuffy, and its seats seemed to have been designed for emaciated dwarfs. But then, lurking below my immediate resentment were regret and the deep melancholy that passing time can bring us. We were approaching now the final week of our visit. I would have welcomed a few more days in Christchurch or a return to Dunedin or Queenstown. I didn't want to leave the South Island for the North Island, which might have more people but had fewer of my new friends. So when the plane began to come down and gave us a glimpse of the well-known tourist resort of Rotorua, the place looked terrible. And Christchurch and Dunedin were already fading like cities seen in a dream.

CHAPTER 10

At Lake Taupo

Though the tall geyser at Rotorua was a charmer, it worked no magic, and during the uncomfortable ride to Taupo one of us was rather cross (Jacquetta) and the other grumpy (me). We knew where we were staying in Taupo – Derek-instructions of course – and it was called *Manuel's* *Beach Resort* and we didn't like the sound of it. Our heavily curtained room seemed close and poky. The fact that we could dine at Manuel's 'Spanish Restaurant' brought no cheer, because even if the food happened to be really Spanish (it wasn't), we had been in Spain in our time and had never admired its cuisine. Still rather cross, still grumpy, we began our unpacking, not briskly but slowly and heavily, as if we had dresses, shirts and pants made of lead. (Here I beg to remind the reader that we were not running around with an over-night bag but with an amount of luggage and its contents to cope with seven weeks, so that unpacking in any small room was no carefree activity: *Where the so-and-so so-and-so am I going to put these?* I can still hear myself demanding.) Then one of us – it must have been Jacquetta – stopped unpacking to pull the curtain away from the french windows. The effect was magical. Manuel, whoever he was, for I never met him, was instantly forgiven. There, a wonderful sight, was the big lake smiling at us, lapping away within a girl's stone-throw. Surely I am right to say that the effect was magical, for it is no accident that lakes appear so often in myths and legends. Lakes this size can suddenly whip up storms – more than

114

once they have terrified me – but it is the union of their placid surfaces with suggestions of strange darkening depths that sets the enchantment to work. Somewhere at the back of our minds we feel as our ancestors did that anything might appear to break that surface, from a pale waving hand and wet-gold tresses to some frightful long-hidden monster.

So here we were, ready to stare ourselves into bewitchment, on the northern shore of the country's largest lake. We had seen it before, of course, high on the viewpoint when we were on our way to the Chateau, weeks ago, but it was far more fascinating down here on the very edge of it. There was a little landing-stage almost opposite our room. In the early morning both shag and cormorant came to perch on it, and from it rather later we fed the ducks. Later still there would be men messing about with boats near or at the landing-stage, and though I never want to join them, I can always smoke a pipe or two just idly watching men mess about with boats. Indeed, I could keep an eye on the lake in a sleepy fashion when there was nothing there but itself, not a man, not a bird, not a boat. We were all right now, capable of enjoying ourselves. The food wasn't bad; no more Spanish than I am but none the worse for that. Derek, who would stay with us until we flew home from Auckland, was on his way up from Wellington.

We had a good driver, Frank Reed, younger than the other drivers, more matey and less inclined to be constantly informative. He was on hand two or three times when I was doing some painting, became infected, and on our final morning with him he produced a curious effort of his own, which I am sure that pretty but intolerant girl in Auckland (next chapter) would have preferred to anything I could do, discovering in it, I have no doubt, a fresh vital primitive. Then again, while the township of Taupo was no urban masterpiece it was more of a genuine little town and less of a tourist trap than I had expected. Having to buy a few things there I had some general chat with two or three shopkeepers and found them inclined to grumble about taxes. As I am one of the world's most insistent and formidable tax-grumblers – the Inland Revenue will never be happy until it has driven me into bankruptcy – I made sympathetic noises, without telling them they little knew what Income Tax could really do to them. Incidentally, I deeply resent having had to hand over a fortune without anybody having once said *Thank you*. Moreover, I still don't understand why almost punitive measures are taken against authors who happen to do fairly well, while property developers, fellows who ruin the look of one city after another, are allowed to get away with millions.

No sooner had Derek arrived than he sought out one Jim Storey, who had a launch in which Jacquetta and Derek went out fishing on the lake, while I was busy painting it. They returned each carrying two large 'rainbow' or salmon trout, which weighed between four and five pounds but somehow looked much larger than that. We ate one of them, but though it was nicely cooked and very pleasant it seemed rather coarse and missed the delicate flavour of our English salmon trout. It was as if the palate had to sacrifice something for this easy fishing and the size of the fish themselves. No doubt New Zealand readers will think I am downright stupid if I announce now that I had been puzzled for the last five weeks because no trout ever appeared on a menu. Here was a country, I kept telling myself, where trout were supposed to be abundant, exceptionally large, and easily fished, yet I had to put up with snapper and something called *tarakihi*. It was not until this very day of Taupo fishing that I learnt that in this country you could eat your own trout or your friends' trout but couldn't go to the market and buy any. *Are you kidding?* I seem to hear the wide boys crying. To which I can only reply that wherever we had been dining, all regulations had been strictly obeyed, and never a trout of any sort had we been offered. In a world now half-crazy with commercialism, where almost everything, including honour and decency, is for sale, New Zealand trout is forbidden the market. You catch it, not buy it.

Now for *Steam*, the prima donna, the star attraction of this thermal area show. In its purest form I fell in love with it, painting it almost with my tongue hanging out. But this must wait. The leading lady must not be discovered at the beginning of the first act. Not that there isn't a charming leading-lady aspect of the geysers, as I suggested earlier. Even so, as a geyser watcher, I wish I had been around between 1900 and 1904 when the Waimangu Geyser, now extinct, went sparkling up to 1,500 feet – the world's supreme fountain. But I do blench a bit at wonderlands (except Alice's) with all their teas and light lunches, souvenirs, films, ice-creams. I don't like their trick of giving every marvel a name, nudging you as you stare at it. I prefer naming them myself or leaving them nameless. The wonderlanders have tamed, harnessed, catalogued, signposted, so many curious scenes that half the wonder or the dread are squeezed out of them. Even so, there are some fine sinister effects, and if I were directing a science-fiction horror film I would want to make use of them.

There are, for example, those muddy hot pools that are not impressive at first sight, but as you stand and stare at their winking and bubbling you begin to feel they are up to no good, that somewhere in their nightmare depths monsters may be growing extra heads and tentacles. They are pools on some other and even worse planet. Then there are the caverns you peer down into, down and down into a hot sulphurous darkness, where there must be some back entrance into Hell. (Dogmatic Christianity, in its less charitable moments, might have been inspired by a sight of some thermal region.) The walls of these caverns favour a green of a most peculiar shade, acid and satanic, that you feel must have arrived out of darkness and never known sunlight. Even when the immediate effect seems pretty enough, mingling as some of the larger pools do a brighter green, various yellows, touches of pink and glimpses of turquoise blue, caught through a steamy haze – like the one I tried in vain to paint – the enduring effect seems hostile, in a faintly diabolical fashion, to our common hopeful or wistful humanity. Planet Earth, it seems in these wonderlands, is signalling from below its disapproval of us. To go from them to a region of pure white steam is like going from the poetry of Edgar Allan Poe to the poetry of Wordsworth.

There is irony here too, at least for somebody like me, inclined to view advanced technology with suspicion. I owed this vision of steam, which I stared at with delight and eagerly painted, to the Wairakei Geothermal Electricity enterprise, in the electrical supply business for the nation. Apparently – which means I know nothing about it – dozens and dozens of bores, some of them going down several thousand feet, tap some unimaginable mass of pressurized steam far below. Somehow – and that is the best I can do – the moisture is taken out and what remains, about a seventh, goes through pipes to a generating station. But that is their concern, not mine. What fascinated and delighted me was all the steam that was set free, everywhere in sight. On all sides it jetted and billowed, floated and faded. It was beautiful. As it came out of the ground it was whiter than a fresh fall of snow, whiter than anything in the world, a pure whiteness turning by comparison all the high clouds into the light grey I used to paint them. Then as it lost energy, floated and began to thin out, various faint tints crept into the whiteness. Finally, as it vanished altogether it seemed to beautify the landscape it revealed, as if the hills and trees and shrubs were newly made and one caught a momentary glimpse of Eden. (What a wonderful idea, even if it never quite worked, Wagner had when he insisted at Bayreuth upon having a *steam curtain*!) I don't know and don't really care how much electric power is generated by the Wairakei geothermal experts, but I do know and greatly care about the peak experience its escaping steam offered me. This cleansed and then illuminated the mind and uplifted the heart.

There were some side-effects, not beautiful but quaint, comic, appealing, in this little world of billowing steam. The one that continually tickled me, whenever it caught my eye, could be discovered on the neighbouring hillsides. Out of the thick foliage up there, well away from the great clouds of steam, would come fairly regular distant puffings, without any clue to their origin. And I never saw them without imagining giants, hidden by the leaves, lolling up there enjoying a quiet smoke. This added a fairy-tale element to the wide scene. The quaint and the comical, typical of so many of these tales, lurked along the edge of beauty. And all this had

been created, as a mere by-product, by something I had often
abused, namely, our advanced technology, to which I could now say
more or less what Wordsworth cried in the end *To the Cuckoo*:

> . . . the earth we pace
> Again appears to be
> An unsubstantial faery place . . .

So long as a little imagination is brought to the scene.

I could have lingered for days and days at Wairakei but I visited it
only once again, and then in very different circumstances. We had
accepted an invitation to attend a dinner at the large and imposing
Wairakei Hotel, where the Association of Booksellers was holding its
Conference. To fulfil this engagement, we had changed our whole
itinerary, going earlier to South Island and returning earlier. There
was a general reason why I was ready to do this, and within this there
was a special reason. First, before we left I was anxious to meet some
New Zealand booksellers, and clearly an afternoon buying books at
Wilkinson's Pharmacy, Queenstown, didn't satisfy that desire.
Secondly, the special reason now, my publishers in London had told
me that I must meet Mr Hedley, who was not a city bookseller and
yet contrived to be one of the most enterprising and knowledgeable
men in the New Zealand book trade. I was also told, after I had
arrived in the country, that I would meet Mr Hedley at this Conference, which he never failed to attend. So our itinerary schedules,
time-tables, Derek-instructions, were juggled around to bring us to
this dinner. But – alas and heigh-ho! – this was the one Conference
Mr Hedley did fail to attend, a family illness keeping him away. And
if these words meet his eye – and I gather that if they don't, then I
have a flop on my hands so far as New Zealand is concerned – I beg to
assure him I was sharply disappointed.

However, there were plenty of other booksellers and their wives, all
smart and bright-eyed; hundreds and hundreds of them, it seemed to
me. No evidence of bad trade and poverty was to be seen, no shiny
frayed suits, no dresses hastily tarted up. Either a great deal of reading
was done in New Zealand or there was a prosperous traffic in

stationery, fountain-pens and fancy goods. (I am not a cynical man, as I might appear to be in that passage, but I *am* an English writer, of long and thick experience.) We were received, with a courtesy that had some warmth in it, by the officers of the Association, elderly men of a scholarly type, who gave me the impression at first that they probably dealt with rare copies of early settlers' memoirs rather than certain plays, novels, essays, coming from England.

However, there came into my possession, along with the agenda and various reports of the Conference, an address given by the President, Mr Gordon Tait, in 1972. It begins, admirably, as follows:

> When I read through the programme for your conference I was almost overwhelmed by the weight of it; the impression I got was one of heaviness, seriousness and earnestness. The emphasis appeared to be on the importance of reading, the responsibility of parents, the responsibility of teachers, and there seemed to me something wrong. I recalled that it is generally assumed illiteracy ceased to be a problem in New Zealand at the turn of the century, yet any librarian or bookseller will tell you that, at most, only about 20 per cent of the community read books. Eighty per cent of non-readers in the community doesn't sound to me very much like a literate society.
>
> Could it be that we are going about things the wrong way? Awareness of the importance of reading and emphasis on the responsibility for encouraging it doesn't seem to have increased the proportion of readers in the community. I suspect that concentration on the importance of reading has turned what can be sheer delight into a tiresome duty.

The title of his address being *Children and Books*, Mr Tait goes on to say that children should be surrounded by books, both at school and at home, to discover their magic for themselves. And most emphatically, it seems, in New Zealand they are not. Down there, Professor McLuhan, prophesying the end of the printed work, is winning.

I wish I had had the chance to go through this ample Conference material before I spoke that night. It would have provided a wide choice of topics. For example, those courses, One, Two and Three altogether, for booksellers' assistants. I buy most of my books from a large bookshop in the West End of London. It has two or three men and a few middle-aged women, who understand what they are doing, surrounded by an indeterminate number (according to the season) of temporary assistants whom I avoid and who only know that they are bewildered and probably underpaid. One competent assistant in a bookshop is worth about eight goggle-eyed auxiliaries. Then again, there is somewhere a mention of bags, and if this means the sort of thing that arrives here every other morning, then I am against them and wish they would disappear. For years and years and years opening parcels of books all the time, I cut some string and put aside some brown paper – and there were the books. Now I may be wrestling ten minutes or so with these confounded bags, typical examples of misapplied ingenuity, scratching myself with spikes and staples, spilling that horrible wood padding, and vainly longing, in this as in other matters, for vanished simplicity. One address I wish I had heard – at 3.20 p.m. on this very Wednesday too – was on *Shoplifting and Store Security* by Detective-Sergeant McWilliams. As it was, just reading here and there in this material, I began to feel somewhat confused. If so few New Zealanders wanted to read a book, let alone own one, why the menace of shoplifting, why the emphasis on security? (Incidentally, *security* is a term I regard with growing suspicion.) Again, if schools in New Zealand are desperately short of books, and most homes haven't any at all, how can the imposing Wairakei Hotel fill its large dining-room with so many prosperous shining booksellers and their smart, bright-eyed wives?

After dinner in that room I was called upon to speak and did so. Though I was cordially received, though everybody afterwards was too polite to chide me or directly express any disappointment, I realized that I had done it again – I had been too short to satisfy my audience. This brings me of course to those cross-purposes I mentioned in the last chapter, now demanding an explanation. The truth is, that as a speaker, and especially as an after-dinner speaker, I had wandered too far away from my own familiar territory. Long ago I decided at home that most speakers go on too long, trying the patience of their hearers. This is particularly true when such people have been wining and dining and long to resume talk with their neighbours at the table. So I determined to be always on the short side, often ending quite abruptly, keeping well away from those 'few last thoughts' that can be so tedious. Then I would be told what a splendid speech I had made and how they wished I had gone on longer. (They didn't, and that is my point.) The comparative brevity, the abrupt surprise ending, were geared, we might say, to the amount of patience possessed by an English audience, and especially a London audience, consisting largely of people who are always hearing other people make speeches.

Certain cities in certain countries – London is one of them and New York is another – could be described as 'centres of impatience', and speakers there, if they are wise, should take this into account. What I forgot is that New Zealand is a long way from any 'centre of impatience', so that its people are ready to settle down and listen cheerfully to longish speeches, probably two or three times the length of any I made. They come to listen and not to get listening over with. Every visiting speaker has come halfway round the globe to talk to them. So let him stand up there and give good measure. No brevity, no artfully abrupt endings wanted, however surprising and welcome they might be to the impatient, half a world away. Priding myself on being a good judge of audiences, I was thousands of miles out when it came to speaking to New Zealand. I must have left behind an exhaust-trail of disappointment, just because I was so ridiculously afraid that audiences down there would run short of patience. And now of course I am sorry.

On Thursday morning we had to leave Taupo for Auckland, Derek driving us. After a farewell look at the lake's early morning show, starring shag-cormorant, duck, and a last stare across the water at the mountains shining on the opposite shore, we began packing quite slowly, no zest in it. The car that Derek had hired for this last journey was loaded up – or down. Off we went. I didn't stop the car in or near

Wairakei, to say goodbye to Steam, not quite human yet but close to achieving a mysterious feminine presence – what was the use? At Rotorua we stopped for lunch, eating in an enormous serve-yourself place which, unlike me, belonged to the future. Again we took to the road, bound non-stop now for Auckland, the end of this and all the other New Zealand journeys.

CHAPTER 11

At Auckland

We were driven straight to the Auckland suburb of Parnell, close to the Boat Harbour, and to the White Heron Hotel and Villas. Jacquetta and I had been allotted one of the villas, very spacious and grand, able to cope if necessary with a fairly large family. Instead of being wedged into one smallish bedroom, we seemed to have rooms galore here and for the first half-hour or so kept wandering from room to room like lost children. From a small balcony at the back of the villa we looked down on the water speckled with scores and scores of yachts at anchor, all longing for the week-end. Out there at Parnell we seemed almost cut off from the city itself, which is one reason why I never really took in Auckland, never accepted it, so to speak, as a character, as I had done the other three cities. We kept going into it or through it but never felt *of it*. The large opulent style of the villa that housed us may have had something to do with this, unconsciously tempting us to adopt that detached attitude so often favoured by the rich, who very frequently don't want to get involved in anything because somebody may soon be asking them for money. (We are not rich.) Moreover, we never seemed to have the time for leisurely exploring, the only way to get to know a city. Being driven through it, this way and that, I always seemed to be impressed by a cheerful and prosperous higgledy-piggledy, yesterday and today all mixed up, and while this was not at all unattractive the city refused to present itself as a place with a

Ocean Beach, Mount Maunganui, by Gaston de Vel

Fishing Boats, Westport, by John M. Crump

Native Bush, Westland, by Peter McIntyre

Ferns, New Zealand Forest, 1851, by Charles Emilius Gold, 1803–71
(*By courtesy of the Trustees of the Alexander Turnbull Library*)

definite character, unlike the South Island cities of Dunedin and Christchurch.

However, my final reason for not really taking hold of this city, not fixing it in the memory, is probably the most convincing. We were now living in the shadow of our impending departure on Sunday night. Our visit was coming to an end. Now one's stock of curiosity is not inexhaustible – at least, mine isn't – and by the time we had reached Auckland my stock, so far as New Zealand was concerned, was running down fast. There will be nothing in this chapter about the evening or night life of Auckland, a sad omission when we remember that this is the largest and wealthiest of the cities. But it is easily explained. First, having done what we undertook to do during the day, we returned to Parnell and our villa, had a bath, got into some different clothes (it was still very warm in Auckland), had a drink, and then were content to walk across to the excellent restaurant, to dine and take it easy. We lacked the enterprise, the *will*, to go out again and explore Auckland at night. Even so if some people had wanted to pull us out, had asked us to dine or to go round sampling this or that, we were not so far sunk into lethargy that we would have refused to stir. But nobody did, not a soul, so that one important aspect of Auckland life is not reported here. For this I refuse to accept any blame. We had had nearly six weeks of constant travel, enquiry, new experience; we were now existing in the shadow of our final departure; we responded during the day to any advance or invitation we received (with Jacquetta, as usual, working harder than I did) and even initiated something with the university, as I shall shortly prove; and if, taking our ease in Parnell, we completely ignored the public or private life of Auckland at night, the fault was not entirely ours.

On Friday morning, I recorded two different TV interviews, and I believe that Jacquetta was similarly engaged. She lunched with her friend, Lady Aileen Fox, who was at the university as Visiting Lecturer in Archaeology and incidently finding her stay in Auckland immensely enjoyable – for which the city gets full marks. Enthusiastic and energetic – how far behind we have left those languid Victorian ladies! – the pair of them went off immediately after lunch to visit

Auckland's volcanic cones. I had gone off to lunch with the officers or committee of the Auckland University Students' Association. I must explain this engagement. Some time before I had read in a newspaper a lively account of a Women's Lib meeting (fervently for, jeeringly against) organized by Auckland students. So these, I decided, were the lads and girls for me. I had lectured to students, among others, in Wellington; I had spent two evenings with academics in Dunedin; I would postpone an encounter with students until I reached Auckland. So I had asked Derek to set up this engagement, beginning with lunch and then going on to talk to and with as many students as cared to attend the session.

The lunch itself, with about a dozen of us eating in a private room in the canteen or refectory, was rather good; and I didn't like to ask if it had been specially ordered for my benefit or if they did themselves as well as this every day. (No steaks when I was up at Cambridge: I used to lunch off a couple of rolls, a piece of cheese, and a glass of Madeira, cheap at that time.) I can't describe my fellow lunchers: they just looked as students now look almost everywhere, with a sprinkling of those beards that proclaim, instead of disguising, their wearers' youth, rather as if the lads were playing charades. Our conversation was polite rather than spirited. But then I had noticed, on my way up to that private room, that on the campus an Abortion Demo was about to be staged, and I felt even then that this would attract the wilder and more eloquent students. And I was right.

Weeks afterwards I received offprints from what I took to be a student paper, called *Happenings*. It seems that Helen Davis, who didn't make herself known to me, reported this occasion, and her account of it is fair if rather sketchy. If there had been any excitement I would add my account to hers. There was no excitement. If I was facing any enthusiastic Maoists, grim Trotskyites, wild anarchists, scornful reactionaries, idiot neo-Fascists, then they kept silent. But then I don't think I was. These were the quiet types; the others must have been preparing the Abortion Demo below. They stared a bit; they listened; they contrived not to yawn. I told them they could ask me any question they liked; but apparently they didn't like, so I was kept talking away from one o'clock to two. I knew as much about what young New Zealand was thinking at two o'clock as I had known at one o'clock.

The report by Helen Davis, to whom I offer my thanks, told me more than all her fellow students did. Let me quote a little of it:

> JBP entered quietly, a small grey-suited man with deep seamed and tucked bags under his eyes, radiating that self-assurance peculiar to a vanishing breed of Englishman; an arrogance beyond arrogance by virtue of being entirely unconscious.
>
> He sat down in the middle of the room and, at his suggestion, the students gathered around, most at a respectful distance. One young man sat himself down beside the visitor and played, rather disconcertingly, with his bare toes throughout the proceedings ...

(I wish I had noticed that young man. He might have provided me with a topic that could have enlivened those proceedings.) But two more quotes, very brief, before I make any comment. When for a moment I did become impatient, I am told I spoke 'in a wondrous gunboats-and-dear-queen voice'. And then, at the end: 'It might amuse him to know, in fact, that several generations of colonials were reared to think of God as being an Englishman rather like himself ...'

Phew! But let vanity have the first word. This small man again! Why? It is true, as those of us who have watched the New Zealand rugger and cricket teams in England know very well, this is a country that produces more than its share of tall heavy-shouldered young men. But I didn't notice any of them that day among Miss Davis's acquaintances, and at 5 ft 9 in. (unless of course I am shrinking fast) and heavily built no students present seemed to be dwarfing me. However, this is a trifle compared with her other mistakes, which tell us far more about one New Zealand girl than they do about me. Why the colonial chip-on-the-shoulder? She writes as if Lord Curzon or Rudyard Kipling had come into the room. Vain I may be; conceited I may be; but arrogant I am not. Instead of belonging to 'a vanishing breed of Englishmen' with 'gunboats-and-dear-queen' voices, I am the very antithesis of this type, having long been an anti-Establishment outspoken radical, with a fairly marked north-country accent that would have kept me out of the Foreign Office if ever I had been daft enough to want to enter it.

Helen Davis, my connection with Imperialist arrogance and gun-boats is about as close as yours to the *Moulin Rouge*. But I have learnt more from you than from your fellow-students at that meeting. And you worry me. You are probably a clever girl; there are some sharp points in your report; but, leaving me out of it (though I can't help wondering what books and plays of mine you can possibly be acquainted with), your ideas of England and the English are fifty years out of date. It is as if you had inherited them from a rebellious grandfather, who wanted to be a New Zealander and not a displaced Englishman. And quite right too, I say. But, Miss Davis, you ought to have moved on from there. You mustn't assume that while New Zealanders have changed, the English haven't. No doubt there may be a few who haven't, and no doubt these few are about my age, into or approaching their eighties. But beware – and this is a common fault – of being entirely hypnotized by the generation gap. In terms of manners and certain tastes the gap may represent a genuine division. So for example you and your friends may enjoy pop music while I and my contemporaries detest it and would rather pay a fine than spend an evening in a discothèque. But then when I was young I was ready to roar out music-hall songs distasteful to my parents. But when we dig deeper and get down to temperaments and character and political and social attitudes of mind, division by the gap won't work. There are timidly conventional types on both sides of it. There are still defiant rebels and radical thinkers on both sides of it. Have a heart! – I was jeering at patronizing Imperialism and all that gunboat-and-dear-queen stuff before you were born. And I don't have that kind of voice, even when impatient. Either you have no ear, Helen Davis, or you have never heard the real dreadful thing.

Still with *Happenings* in front of me, I have been reading an account of an interview with Jacquetta. It is not too bad. (Here I must add that when people imagine, as I think so many of them do, that interviewing is easy, they are quite wrong. Even if shorthand is there to help, it is still quite difficult.) The interviewer merely signs herself *P.R.* so I can't address her by name. And while she didn't do a bad job, she did begin with an enormous gaffe, describing Jacquetta:

> She is a coolly elegant county lady, the well-cut suit and pearls type, who has spent much of her life amid the academic cloisters of Oxford and Cambridge. (Her father was Sir Frederick Gowland Hopkins, the discoverer of vitamins.)

Come off it, P.R.! We know that county lady, the well-cut suit (or 'twin-set') and pearls type, with all her dogs that have to be walked daily, with her high, hardish, *staring* kind of voice, her various snobberies, her garden-party Tory opinions, her suspicion of any wide-ranging sympathies, her lack of imagination. It is a familiar type, though it is also a type that is on its way out. (Put this down to heavy taxation, shortage of domestic servants, lack of funds to maintain the old country-house style of life, the rapidly changing outlook and manners of her young.) And Jacquetta bears about as close a resemblance to this type as I do to any player in the Tottenham Hotspur football team.

My wife is a well-known and highly respected archaeologist who is at least half a poet, as her major works testify. She has a quiet manner and may be thought at first to be shy; but in fact she is quite fearless and can if necessary be very outspoken. She is capable of standing up in a hall largely filled with scientists and telling them to their faces that she is dead against their 'reductionism'. At a time when future county ladies were 'coming out' as debs, Jacquetta was probably grubbing about in archaeological diggings or exploring reptile-infested ruins. One of my favourite images of her I had to take from television, simply because she was marching and I never march for any cause, having done my share of that boring exercise as an infantryman in the First War. But one year after another she could be seen striding along in the front rank of the great C.N.D. Aldermaston marches, wearing a large slouch hat and looking not unlike a particularly handsome Confederate general in the American Civil War. *County lady* my foot! But now back to New Zealand. I wouldn't say,

'Jones is a typical Otago back-country man' or 'Mrs Brown is the Auckland upper-bracket over-stuffed-suite type', because I wouldn't know what I was talking about, I would be trying to make a flip comment while my feet were eighteen inches above the ground. However, while intending a friendly and smiling rebuke, I seem to have not only made my point but hammered and banged it home. So here is England's favourite expression: *Sorry – sorry!*

That Friday afternoon, as soon as the students and I had gratefully reached 2 p.m. I had to make my way to the War Memorial Museum. I would have paid it a visit anyhow before I left Auckland, but this Friday afternoon engagement had been fixed by an invitation, which arrived at my end almost sounding like a command, from Sir Henry Kelliher, who would be there himself to receive me. The Kelliher Art Trust was presenting a Joint Exhibition of paintings by official Australian and New Zealand War Artists, which he would be pleased to show me. I had learnt already that Sir Henry was not only a successful and wealthy brewer and financier but was also a generous patron of the visual arts – so long as they were reasonable and behaved themselves. Approached through a fine park and raised well above all neighbouring ground, the War Memorial Museum, with its eight great pillars and colonnade entrance, is very impressive indeed. It offers one, among a great many other things, a genuinely solemn large-scale Hall of Memories, a be-flagged Shrine, together with an inscription above its entrance that is worth quoting:

> The whole earth is the Sepulchre of famous men. They are commemorated not only by columns and inscriptions in their own country but in foreign lands also, by memorials graven on stone but in the hearts of men.

I for one prefer not to think of the earth as a sepulchre but to imagine it as a green globe, often dark and dangerous but also often illuminated by what famous men have thought and felt and done so that they shine in our memory. But then what we have here, outside in the park as well as in this building, is a vast memorial to the fallen.

It is only the largest of many impressive memorials, and both direct observation and photographs have shown me that New Zealand laments and salutes its dead soldiers far more generously and lavishly than Britain does. Where an English town might have a rather miserable little monument, a New Zealand town of the same size would have decided on something far larger and more impressive. This is not because the British have been less closely attached to sons and brothers, husbands and sweethearts. No difference can be found on this level. We must look for it somewhere else. Now the First War, the supreme killer, was almost on our doorstep. During the big battles a Kentish mother or wife could have put her head out of the bedroom window and heard the guns shaking the southern sky. She was almost on the edge of Death's harvesting. The days could be grim and the nights worse. But I can't help feeling that when the news of a fatal casualty struck a New Zealand family, it must have been far worse still. The young men had sailed away into nowhere or the un-imaginable, and something on the other side of the world had killed them or left them dying 12,000 miles from home. The very remote-ness of the country entered here to heighten the pride but also to deepen and embitter the tragedy of their loss. And this is why, to my way of thinking, New Zealand has larger and more impressive war memorials.

There was plenty of good honest work by the official Australian and New Zealand War Artists. I was touched to find, among the Australian painters of the First War, work by George Lambert. Not that I knew him, though he had spent many years in London, but his son, Maurice, the sculptor, had been a friend of mine, and I was at least casually acquainted with his other son, Constant, the brilliant musician. Both had died far from easy deaths years before they ought to have done: this was one of those unusually gifted but tragic families. As for war paintings and drawings in general, it is my belief that too many of them insist upon showing us action – the charge of the Lancers or artillery-men loading their guns. But if you have known war at first-hand – and this is particulary true of the First War – it is its terrible landscape, the earth caught in a nightmare, that haunts the imagination. For this reason apparently simple drawings and sketches by artists like Paul and John Nash, perhaps glimpses of the horrible no-man's-land seen from the trenches, with its tree stumps and raped earth, are remembered when far more elaborate studies of men in action are forgotten.

But I have to admire the way in which Sir Henry Kelliher has brought his genuine passion for Australian and New Zealand landscape into his business. I have in front of me now, for it is one of the things I insisted upon having sent home after me, his fine large Dominion Breweries Calendar for 1973, far superior to the many pictorial calendars I receive. Its paintings, two or three of them old, the rest contemporary, are exceptionally well reproduced, and its final page offers us little photographs of the artists and some biographical notes – altogether a handsome and sensible job. I hope living New Zealand landscape men, to whom I am indebted for some work reproduced in this book, will forgive me if I add that the page in this calendar I return to most frequently represents an Australian painter, John Loxton, who died in 1970 – a name, I am sorry to say, quite new to me. His *Australian Drover on the Road to Wagga Wagga* seems to me a triumph of impressionism in light, colour, tone, atmosphere; and is at least as good in its way as our Nolan, which shows us a mysterious Ned Kelly against an equally mysterious ghost-tree outback. Nolan may have had his due, but it is high time we English, now that we are no longer 'arrogant' gents, made a fuss about the painters and poets of Australia and New Zealand.

Jacquetta represented the Priestleys in the extensive and richly varied ethnological and anthropological departments of the War Memorial Museum. I did take a respectful peep at the tremendous Maori collection, which I gather is justly famous. Some New Zealand readers, haunted by the country's Maori past (as I suggested much earlier), may feel strongly that in chapter after chapter I have ignored, either deliberately or quite blindly, the Maori element in the life of the two islands, and especially the North Island. Apart from our early encounter with the two feather-cloak ladies, I have never taken a look at the Maoris. Is this sheer laziness, to which I have already pleaded guilty? No, I don't feel it is. I have deliberately and not blindly ignored the Maori. If I had in hand a big book about New Zealand, then the Maori would come in all over the place, not only historically but also as what I suspect to be a growing or deepening influence on the more sensitive aspects of New Zealand life and national character. Given more experience and research, I would have a shot at explaining how, largely through the influence of the unconscious, the warmth and sensuousness of South Pacific life, of the Polynesian tradition, began to invade and fertilize the frozen remains of the old New Zealand puritanical habit of mind. However, I have neither the opportunity nor the knowledge such a big book demands: I am simply writing a fairly brief, informal and very personal account of a six weeks' visit; and even to begin dealing fairly with the Maori would have lengthened this account and even then would probably have left it lopsided. So I have more or less ignored them; staring at canoes and carvings and then moving on to my next encounter with New Zealanders who are technically white even though they are pink or brown. For this I don't propose to apologize: I have done too much apologizing already.

As we had no day engagement for Saturday, we cheerfully accepted Sir Henry's invitation to lunch with him and some of his family at a Dominion Breweries hotel, and then to discover what he had done with his property, Puketutu Island, formed by one of those many volcanic cones. This is now connected with the mainland by a causeway, so that we rode there in comfort. It was clear from the first that our host shared his passion for landscape competitions and awards with an equal passion for his island. It was also clear, although we were getting along nicely, that he and I represented opposite poles of the human temperament. Like so many successful wealthy men of business he had a very marked possessive streak in him; he enjoyed owning things and then striving hard to improve them and then displaying and explaining what he had done. Such a man needs an island whereas I don't think I would accept an island even as a gift. So far as owning things is concerned I am more than halfway towards a Buddhist monk. Except so far as they contribute to ease and comfort, possessions seem to me a nuisance, and I fancy that if I had ever inherited an

estate I would have spent my days reading and smoking in a moulder-
ing library, allowing the whole estate to drift into ruin. Sir Henry
would have improved it about 1,000 per cent.

This is what he must have done with his island, with an enduring
passion for improvement that I could never imitate but can respect.
From roads and paths to flowers, shrubs, trees, and from them to
horses and cattle, his sharp eye and pointing finger have let nothing
escape his attention and the result is notable indeed. He is excusably
proud of his island, but I think his pride and joy rise to a peak when
his racehorses are brought out. And here, I am afraid, though politely
admiring, I let him down. To begin with, I am no racegoer nor any
kind of horseman, though in my time and in a clumsy apprehensive
fashion I have ridden horses, both in England and Arizona; but
always without developing any affection for the beasts. The truth is,
the only horses I have truly regarded with love, from boyhood
onwards, are the wonderful great cart-horses, Shire horses, Per-
cherons, and their like, at once mighty and gravely patient, so unlike
the neurotic creatures at the other end of the breeding scale. Sometimes I have caught a look in the eyes of these huge and strangely
noble animals that suggested a dim ancestral remembrance of the
time when their kind was so precious because it could carry massively
armoured knights into battle, like so many tanks today. But I said not
a word of this to Sir Henry, his eyes gleaming at his racehorses. But
when the island had been thoroughly explored and admired and we
sat down to our whisky – for he was a faultless host – he and I perhaps
exchanged rather too many words, though never heatedly. But we
began to range over the wide political scene, to consider the state of
the world, together with some racial questions, and then – alas for
the end of a pleasant day – the difference in temperament and outlook
became uncomfortably manifest. There was a gap here not to be
bridged by a common enthusiasm for landscape paintings. However,
we parted amiably and our thanks for his hospitality and all the
trouble he had taken were quite sincere.

Back at the villa I was delighted to welcome R. M. Lockley, who
had brought along an inscribed copy of his book *Man Against Nature*.

Ever since our first arrival in Auckland, nearly six weeks before, when he and I had talked on the telephone and he had told me about this book, I had tried in vain to secure a copy of it. The publishers, Messrs Reed, ought to bring it out now as a superior paperback. (I like superior paperbacks, which have in fact stiffish covers, and often prefer them to the original cloth-bound editions of the same books.) I have already described why Lockley wrote *Man Against Nature,* and all I need add here is that it is full of what is missing in this book of mine, namely, a closely observant and intimate account of the New Zealand natural scene. I don't mean that I go through life without ever noticing a bird, a tree, a flower, but I don't know enough and so rarely write about them. Mr Lockley's rather dry manner tends to conceal his passionate concern for the natural scene and the lives of its creatures. As so often happens, this inner heat below the cool surface has prevented him from ageing fast. It is usually the men without compelling interests and enthusiasms who grow old before their time. So though it must be well over thirty-five years since I saw him last, when he was still living on the little island of Skokholm off the Welsh coast, he seemed hardly to have changed at all. Perhaps his freedom from the worst signs of ageing is a magical gift from his beloved seabirds.

We spent Sunday morning, our last morning in New Zealand, visiting the Auckland City Art Gallery, very sensibly open at this time. Its lively director, American, to our surprise, introduced one of his young assistants clever enough to have won a fellowship or scholarship that would shortly take her to London. She was an attractive girl, but like many another her age blazingly intolerant. She offered the exact reverse of Sir Henry Kelliher. The landscape he praised and rewarded were to her just a load of old rubbish. Anything that made her jump with excitement would seem to him so much impudent gimmickry. Unknown to her, for I had neither the time nor the inclination to explain, I occupied a middle or neutral position. I had been looking for a few New Zealand landscapes – and I seem to remember she was snootily aware of this – because by having them reproduced here I could give readers outside the country some idea of what it looked like. Along the way I had noticed, rather hastily I admit, a good deal of strictly contemporary and *avant garde* art, without horror but also without being immediately impressed. (If I had seen anything half as good as the later work of de Stael, for example, poised so wonderfully between representation and abstraction, at once I would have been asking questions about the artist.) But going briskly through one gallery room after another is no way to judge painting in various unfamiliar styles. You have to give yourself time to discover if the artist really has something to say to you. I wasn't entirely unfamiliar with abstract art; I had even tried it. When I was still messing about with oils, I had attempted a number of abstracts (one of them isn't too bad) before deciding that this method – in the words of one of Nancy Mitford's characters – 'wasn't madly me'.

There is irony in the modern world's response to its arts. The very people who praise them for being 'disturbing' are already too much disturbed themselves. The complacent people who might benefit from some disturbance ignore all such work. And just when toleration would help enormously, both sides are far too intolerant. There can be live-and-let-live in the arts too. If I choose to paint *gouaches* as if I belonged to the *avant garde* of 1863, that is my affair, and I don't do anybody any harm, especially as I am not marketing my work at the expense of more interesting artists. Life in this world is sufficient of a dog-fight without turning the arts into bones of contention. They are to be enjoyed, to be attempted and appreciated on many different levels, and don't exist to be fought over. The trouble is, that too many enthusiasts, like the attractive but intolerant girl in the City Art Gallery, assume that the arts are going somewhere, on their way to some final Elysium. It follows therefore that painters of conventional landscapes are lagging behind, perhaps blocking the road, while the *avant garde* painters, true to their name, are hurrying on and on, taking themselves – and us if we have the sense to see it – nearer and nearer to the mysterious but inevitable goal, the entrance to the Promised Land of Art. And this of course is nonsense. The arts aren't going anywhere; they are simply changing, rather like people offering us different dances in the same place.

One thing I did on my last afternoon was to reply to a letter from a man who had something to do with the Auckland Festival of the Arts. He told me I ought to stay until May, when it would burst upon the city. I expressed my regret that this would not be possible. What I didn't go on to say was that I seemed to have arrived in one New Zealand city after another either too late or too early for its festival; and I couldn't help feeling, simply as a visitor, that a constant steady diet of the arts might be preferable to hunger and then one annual huge feast of them. Perhaps I was wrong to feel this. Perhaps there were too many local factors and considerations I couldn't take into account. But then I wasn't in a good state of mind, at least not one I ever like being in – all divided, with too many changing lights and shades. Here I was, packed to go home, and I have never been in a place yet where I didn't look forward to going home. You might say I go away to come home. And yet – and yet – I was within a few hours of leaving Auckland – and indeed New Zealand – for ever; and I hadn't seen enough, I didn't know enough. I gave myself a rather stiff drink, which is something I rarely do unless my mind is feeling at ease. All that a potent drink does to a divided mind is to heighten and strengthen the divisions, with the changing lights and shadows brighter and darker than before. I went out to the little balcony at the back of our villa and stared at the harbour, which was still magnificent but said nothing to me, not being on speaking terms with a visitor who wasn't a yachtsman. I tried the other side of the villa, standing at its entrance as if I were waiting for somebody – perhaps a messenger from Auckland, not even visible from here, to explain it to me. Before I relit my pipe I could almost taste as well as smell the early evening air, and it was richly subtropical, closer to Tangier than to Bournemouth. A few large cars went creeping and purring up to the hotel entrance across the road; nothing else seemed to happen.

But time of course is always happening. With Derek still in charge, we were on our way to the airport. We were in the airport, a Sunday night airport. I was telling myself what joyless occasions we have contrived for ourselves in this modern world. I had been in ships and trains that had moved off in a tragi-comic carnival of tears, laughter, cheers, wavings, drunken bawdy jokes, piercing last messages, with human nature on the boil. But now airports seem to exist in the desiccating atmosphere of advanced technology; they suggest in a glum fashion a political crisis only known to the secret police; they are all of them behind an Iron Curtain; and not only is human nature not encouraged to expand, it is barely allowed to exist, and we begin to feel apologetic because we are still people and not parcels. It is typical of airports and the modern world that after a long delay, during which we begged poor Derek in vain to leave us for his bed, suddenly, almost violently, Jacquetta and I were disjoined from him, rather as if somebody were under arrest; and the last – perhaps the very last – glimpse I had of him as I turned at the bottom of the stairs, his face was all bewilderment hardening into outrage. He ought to have adopted my rule, which has long been dead against seeing anybody off at an airport, now part of a world governed by computers, a world in which messy human beings, with their flowers and kisses, tears and laughter, hopeful last messages and quivering lips, are a nuisance.

CHAPTER 12

Musing over two remote islands

Two long night flights on the way home offered me a chance to think about New Zealand – or at least, when not interrupted, to wander into reveries concerning it. And a brief account of the journey will not remove us too far from the subject of this chapter. We took the Air New Zealand Sunday flight from Auckland to Los Angeles because only on that flight the fuelling stop was at Tahiti. I knew from too many reports that Tahiti was no longer the unspoilt island where I had stayed for a month, between steamers, over forty years ago, when it had been closer to Gauguin than to American Express. But I wanted to see the fantastic shape of it emerging in the early morning sunlight, and I felt that Jacquetta would find this entrancing, as indeed she did. But when we landed at the airport – *an airport on Tahiti!* – and had to remain there because we would be off again in an hour, we found it crowded with tourists, mostly American, apparently just milling around and beginning to sweat. And what I soon noticed was that the Tahitians, especially the young men and the girls, were no longer all broad smiles. I don't say they looked sullen and rebellious. But the smiles had gone; they were no longer enjoying their indolent and carefree island life; now they were busy, in business, in the tourist trade. We had left behind us, in New Zealand, far more smiles.

Very sensibly we had decided to break the journey by spending two nights at Santa Monica. And we were back – see Chapter One – with Graeme Eskrigge again, calm, courteous and helpful as ever but, being plagued by some mysterious ailment, allowing his ironic gleam to take on a sardonic tinge, as if observing this travel fuss through the window of a monastic retreat. To our surprise we enjoyed Santa Monica, which had now cleared all traffic out of its best shopping street, turning it into a leisurely flowery promenade and defying the canons of automobile worship. This seemed to us progress as against American *prog-ress*, the deepening nightmare. Then we boarded an American Jumbo jet ready for the non-stop Polar flight to London. Through the night, reverie was possible though frequently inter-rupted by loud speeches. We might have been back at school on prize-giving day, not roaring through the dark, six or seven miles above illimitable icefields, longing for another drink or two and not for more loud words over the loud speakers. At last – Heathrow, which seemed to imagine that what we needed now was a long walk – and every year they get longer – towards home. Here at home there has been more reverie, some musing, even a few real thoughts, all on the mixed subject of New Zealand and ourselves and the world.

In my first chapter I needed a final answer to that question, 'Why New Zealand?' And here it is, though I have some way to go yet before supplying solid buttresses for my answer. But the people who asked that question – and some of them had visited New Zealand – believed that New Zealand was not only very far away but also that it was quite unimportant. But I had a hunch even then that they were wrong about this unimportance. On my return I felt certain that New Zealand is very important – and, strange though it may seem, very important to us all. It is a special place in a special situation. But this cannot remain a bare assertion. Enquiry, observation, argument are needed.

In passing I remember what friends, who had paid very brief visits themselves, told me to expect in that remote region. For example: 'Nobody waits at table there. You have to help yourself all the time.' Not true, far from it, and a pity in a way because I nearly always enjoy helping myself. Again: 'After lunch on Friday every healthy New

Cowdie [Kauri] Forest on the Wairoa River, Kaipara, 1840,
by Charles Heaphy, 1822–81 *(By courtesy of the
Trustees of the Alexander Turnbull Library)*

The Meeting of the Artist with the Wounded Chief Hongi, Bay of Island,
November 1827, at Korarareka [now Russell], by Augustus Earle, 1793–1838
(By courtesy of the Trustees of the Alexander Turnbull Library)

Christchurch Town Hall: the Auditorium *photographed by Robin Smith*

Christchurch Town Hall:
views of the exterior
photographed by Martin Barriball

Zealand man vanishes from his home for the week-end, to go sailing or fishing or shooting in the mountains.' And if this had been true I would have found both North and South Island filled with exasperated or deeply frustrated wives (surrounded by disappointed children) whereas in fact New Zealand women seemed to me far less dis-satisfied than so many I had encountered in America, Canada, Australia. Then there was the chorus of actors, far out on tour down there and missing Shaftesbury Avenue. 'A beautiful country but very dull people, old boy, bloody dull!'

No doubt there are plenty of dull people in New Zealand, and I may have met a few of them. But outside some small circles in various countries, I don't remember having the luck to be sitting at table, night after night, with witty conversationalists or challenging philo-sophers. There are dull people everywhere – and indeed we are all dull to somebody – and for my part I prefer amiable and cheerful dullards, not uncommon in New Zealand, to aggressive chip-on-the-shoulder types, not uncommon in Australia, or the conceited relentless bores found among important personages throughout the English-speaking world. Possibly some visitors may react against a certain complacency carried like a badge by some middle-aged middle-income New Zealanders. For reasons I shall suggest later, I believe this to be superficial, quite shallow and without roots, put on to disguise feelings that are very different.

However, there is a special reason why actors – and similar urban visitors – have told us that New Zealand is dull. People of this kind are generally susceptible to the glamorous. And in the sense in which I am using the term, New Zealand is entirely without glamour. Its cities are too small, looking like so many suburbs when compared with *real cities*, huge, monstrous and cruel yet dazzling, fascinating, richly rewarding, mixing fabulous luxury with filth and degradation, disgraceful and yet wildly romantic in their promise and mystery. (It is significant that New Zealand youngsters who believe they have talent have no sentimental feeling about Britain itself – no more of that 'home' baloney for them – yet cannot resist the vast magnet of London.) Again, there is glamour where there are fantastically different standards and styles of living, where wealth and privilege parade untroubled before poverty and despair, where there are hovels not far from the gates of great mansions, where wicked men flourish together with the girls whose beauty and impudence have taken them out of the gutter to bathe in milk or wine and to blaze with diamonds. But now I have gone sliding back into the manner of nineteenth-century novelettes. Can New Zealand offer glamour in strictly contemporary terms?

No, it can't. A London or New York fashionable, big-name-show-biz columnist would run out of material on his first day in Auckland, Wellington or Christchurch. Where would he find the names that carry neon lights around with them? Where are the restaurants and night-clubs for the jet set and the Beautiful People? Or the parties, perhaps in fancy dress, that make international news? Or the first nights and the film premières and the spring or autumn fashion shows? Who in the North or the South Island is really *In, With It, Making It*? – not one. Where, for that matter, is luxury itself, the real monstrously expensive self-indulgent thing? From a masculine point of view, I say nowhere in this country. The only caviare it offered me was a cheap fake, probably eggs of whitefish treated with charcoal and seasoning. Wine lists were unambitious, never dreaming of any great occasion. If there were any good cigars on sale anywhere, I never found them – and I tried hard enough. Why, the mere raw materials of the glamorous life were lacking in such a dead level of bungalows and TV snacks. We have to admit that glamour is something New Zealand can't offer. But then we might ask ourselves if we really want glamour, especially if and when something more satisfying than glamour might be on offer.

Nobody must imagine though that the country's rural community exists in a twentieth-century Arcadia. The men who swarm into the pubs near the big sheep stations, men who treat one another not to pints but great jugs of beer, would have no place in a charming pastoral. When they have to be responsible for thousands of sheep, men are not likely to be so many 'gentle shepherds'. They are not deliberately cruel but they can easily become shockingly callous, seeing living creatures in their care as so much merchandise. So I received, while I was out there, letters of protest and a number of press cuttings, denouncing the way in which stock to be slaughtered could be left for days without food and water, the lack of shade or shelter on pastures where trees had been sacrificed for timber, rough-and-ready rapid shearing that left cuts and sores behind it, the dangerous inoculation of cattle with rusty, blunt needles, and even the sale of beef in New Zealand that had already been rejected by countries, notably America, that maintained a higher standard. The story of the deer does not make comforting reading: first they were deliberately introduced, most unwisely as it turned out, as game animals for sport; hunting them, often from helicopters, turned into slaughter, with wild shooting endangering farmers' stock; and now live fawns are more valuable than venison so that scores of the little creatures are captured and sent away. A trade in fawns and factory-farming methods for sheep and cattle do not suggest we are back in Arcadia.

However, it is a mistake to imagine that New Zealanders are mostly farmers. Over 77 per cent of the population now live in urban areas, and I hope, for reasons that will appear later, this percentage will not increase. But while there exists a rough-and-tough element among New Zealanders – and the rugger field can suggest this – the statistics of serious crimes, too serious to be dealt with in magistrates' courts, are very different from those in Britain and America. There has been a slight increase but nothing like the shocking percentages, especially of crimes with violence, that now disturb the British and, above all, the American public. The modest size of the cities, allowing reasonable living space, must have something to do with this, for men denied this space – and particularly hot-tempered men – soon begin to feel frustrated and this feeling may seek release in violence. (This can also be true of children and teenagers living in high-rise new housing estates, seeking revenge on society through vandalism, a rage to be destructive.) Experiments have proved that creatures like rats, when crowded together and deprived of their own living space, will either fiercely attack one another or lose all sense of a satisfactory rat-existence. Though men can put up with more and for a longer time, they will reach angry frustration or despair sooner or later.

Possibly another reason why New Zealand's serious crime figures don't go bounding up is that it has had less than its share of potentially criminal riff-raff. Except perhaps during the earliest whaling days and then the temporary Gold Rush of the 1860's, it has never had other societies' rejects swarming in. Its immigrants have rarely included many of the defeated and the embittered. It does not welcome one and all, and, as I shall shortly argue, it is quite right not to do so. But now what about the country's admirable welfare arrangements? Do they help to keep these crime figures from soaring? Reluctantly – for I believe in welfare – I doubt it, if only because Britain as a Welfare State has produced more and more criminals – and very vicious criminals too, many of them. But there is something else, and it must not be dismissed as being too fanciful, even if it does partly return us to the subject of glamour.

It is this – that the atmosphere of vast rich cities like London and New York breeds violent crime as no urban life in New Zealand does. Wealth is flaunted in these cities. The gap between people with too much money and people with too little is monstrous. Bitter envy is all too common. Robbery itself may be almost a traditional way of life, designed to make a living at other people's expense. But the all-too-frequent *robbery with violence*, almost always avoided by the old professional burglar or for that matter the occasional sneak-thief, may be coolly and elaborately organized but the men who carry out the plan, using violence when it may not even be necessary, could be driven by emotion, hot with envy and hatred. Now obviously some people in New Zealand are much better off than others, but what does not exist there is this particular big-city atmosphere. I may be writing out of ignorance but I find it hard to imagine, let us say, a Christchurch East End group grimly planning to loot a Christchurch West End through armed robbery. Theft and assault there may be, and indeed rape (surprisingly frequent, I thought, though the N.Z. press may play it up), but the figures of serious crime were not mounting and mounting, all in an over-heated atmosphere of false glamour, a contempt for social values, envy and brutal greed. Out of its small and modest cities, where there is no flaunting of wealth and possibly little desire *for more money at all costs*, New Zealand has not created that atmosphere yet, and I hope with all my heart it never will.

It has only to treble the size of its cities to run into trouble. I am no longer thinking now about crime statistics; I am thinking about over-crowding, pollution, traffic problems, and the disappearance of an easy style of living. These cities would exist in a different atmosphere. The proportion of honest folk with quiet minds to riff-raff (on all levels) would rapidly decline. Bump up the population again and soon it might be dangerous to walk the streets at night. And during the day the smiles and friendly greetings would have long gone.

Treble the whole population – to please the industrialists, the advertising men and salesmen, the people who believe they need more and more things to be truly happy – and New Zealand would be just another victim of a civilization that is in a fast car without a driver, rushing towards catastrophe on the motorways to the land of lost content. New Zealand will no longer be a special place; it will be just another place a far way off. It will no longer be in a special situation; it will be in the usual situation, grimly familiar to the rest of us. Its lakes and rivers will be poisoned; its mountains will stonily await final disaster; its clear sunlight and pure air will seem to belong to some almost mythical past. After some artful propaganda, followed by two or three wrong government moves, all this could happen – and then be irreversible.

Such propaganda could succeed and those bad decisions be taken just because, as I have already suggested, much of the apparent com-placency is undermined by a deep uneasy feeling, sometimes close to panic. This whisper in the dark says that New Zealand is too remote, too far 'out of it' and unregarded, and therefore must develop itself on safe familiar lines. And it is not just a matter of more industry, more people with jobs, more money, more things. What about Defence? Here one can only reply that 3,000,000 people who believe in themselves and what they are doing, like the Israelites, might prove to be a harder nut to crack than, say, 12,000,000 who have lost that belief and wonder where they are drifting. With respect, as the politicians like to say, I feel that more New Zealanders should have a stronger faith in their country both as it is and as it could be developed while keeping its essential character. This returns me to my statement, as yet unjustified, that I see it as a special place in a special situation.

I may have said enough along the way to establish the special place. However, a few scattered points for emphasis will do no harm. Here were islands that seemed to remain unchanged from the dawn of time as fantastic bird sanctuaries, ranging from busy little creatures able to fertilize plants like so many bees to families of wingless birds including moas twelve feet high. There were lizards looking like diminished descendants of the vanished dinosaurs, but no snakes, crocodiles, alligators, and no serious pests of any sort; and not a single mammal had landed here. Though sternly mountainous, volcanic in places, lashed often by rainstorms, it was a kind of antediluvian Eden, already archaic long before the myths and parables of Genesis were assembled. Men arrived far later here than anywhere else on earth except the South Polar regions. When the first men, the Maoris, did come, they were too busy fighting and eating each other and enjoying interminable debates in their meeting-houses, to do much lasting damage. It was of course the white man – the world's most reckless spoiler – who in a century and a half of bush burning, over-grazing, failure to harness the water supplies, threatened the lasting fertility of the country and brought its ecology close to ruin. That ardent and eloquent naturalist, R. M. Lockley, has described this melancholy regress in his *Man Against Nature*, though he finally admits that the authorities are at last creating watchful councils and measures for conservation.

The primordial scene that Captain Cook and his men must have known has largely vanished. Determined to create another Britain in the South Pacific, the early settlers – and indeed their successors – brought in myriads of seeds and cuttings. The triumph of this policy is responsible for a wonderland effect. At one moment I could look around and almost believe I was back in Warwickshire, but then not long afterwards I could be staring at giant ferns, strange trees and shrubs out of some lost world. The same settlers brought in dogs and pet cats whose progeny became the country's first marauding wild animals. (And rabbits, food and fun at first, ended as a ravenously devouring menace.) But while I was there I never caught sight of a wild dog or cat, knew that no undergrowth concealed the smallest snake, never had to wonder about mosquitoes, and, while painting many hours outdoors, for once never received a bite from the flies that alighted on my hands just as if even they were still working under Eden rules. No wonder that young Sam Butler – enterprising enough but surely no hero – could go off on his horse to survey unknown territory, making his way all the time through pre-Adamite vegetation and seeing and hearing birds that the rest of the world had never known. A special place indeed! – then and even now, when huge electric power plants may be releasing steam that drifts across the remains of forests hundreds of millions of years old.

Now for the special situation. This is rather complicated because it has more than one meaning and can be looked at in several different ways. We have already seen that the country's ecology has only just been narrowly saved from complete and final disaster. One wrong move now and the healthy relationship between men and land and living-space – which to my mind still exists in New Zealand – could be destroyed, never to be restored. A fairly immediate choice will have to be made between, on the one hand, more industry, more and more people, more wealth, more power of a sort, but all of it threatening the quality of life; and, on the other hand, a community hardly any larger or richer than it is now, with no spectacular 'progress' for public relations to boast about. But this could be a society determined not simply to maintain the present quality of life but to deepen and heighten it, perhaps starting to create a new civilization. And if I am right in believing that this is the choice the country must make, then nobody can deny that it finds itself in a special situation.

I feel compelled to add here that no New Zealander has asked for my advice, but then a man who has worked in his impudent profession as long as I have insists upon giving advice without being asked. At a pinch I am ready to declare that for the next five years or so New Zealand should bar all immigration – except for any young relatives of mine and for a hundred-odd French, Italians, Swiss to take over its restaurants and hotels and perhaps a few shops that could import some missing luxuries. With more underlying gravity I would advise my New Zealand friends – and this should come as no surprise if they have read the rest of this book – to beware of Americanization and Tourism.

Is America all wrong then? Not entirely but it does usually export the worst and not the best of its ideas, habits, styles of living. Moreover, America had to tackle a problem that never challenged the rest of us. It had to turn into responsible American citizens the hordes of Central and East European peasants that arrived, hopeful but bewildered, in New York. For their sake a great deal had to be simplified and standardized. (Language suffered throughout society because its terms became blurred, lacking exact definition. So, for example, *fight* was for any kind of disagreement and *bug* for any sort of insect.) New Zealanders, unlike Americans, had no excuse for spelling *right* 'rite', nor for calling *petrol* 'gas', a far looser term, for there can be gas on sale that is not petrol. Harder to pinpoint but even more important are various advertising and salesmanship devices and tricks that are among America's more dubious exports. One of these I described and denounced earlier, namely, continual piped-music. I will admit at once that Britain and indeed all Western Europe are among the victims of Americanization, but then I am still arguing that New Zealand is a special place in a special situation, and therefore should watch its behaviour.

Now for a howl of protest, for if there is something else that should be watched and carefully considered – it is the tourist trade. This will seem almost like blasphemy in many quarters. Among hard-won national profits, tourism is the rose in bloom. Or, as people used to say, it is money for jam. Let the package tours, bigger every year, come rolling in. Hasn't New Zealand natural marvels to offer that old tourist goals like Italy and Greece cannot match? It has indeed, but, unlike the familiar packaged places where tip-hungry types abound, it is new, innocent, naïve, still friendly and not yet artfully predatory – again, a special place. By all means let it welcome and handsomely lodge and feed the traveller, especially if it takes the right decisions and transforms itself into an important social experiment. If there must be tourists, to be whisked from Waitomo's caves to Rotorua's thermal displays, from Mount Cook to Milford Sound, then there must be tourists, for they can hardly be forbidden to land or be turned back at airports. But it is a very different matter to work at transforming tourism into a major national industry. This would make the country a special place of the wrong sort, a show place catering for idle minds, sooner or later beginning to corrupt a large section of its people, giving what were once decent little towns a false façade to hide their dollar traps, creating a style of life that would be mostly pretence and in which the only reality would be the pursuit of easy money. What was once a friendly innocence would be lost in greed and cynicism. It has happened elsewhere; it could happen here. As we shall see, I believe that New Zealand could be very important indeed, but not if it is chiefly important to travel agents and their 'carefree' customers.

As a special place in a special situation, New Zealand could be of immense importance to a world that now rarely gives it a thought. This can be readily understood as soon as we begin to consider what it can offer. First we must realize that it has already a remarkable record for advanced social legislation, for the elaborate organization of welfare services, on the basic principle – and now I quote its own *Pocket Digest of Statistics* – 'that people should contribute according to their means and receive benefits according to their needs'. And this does not mean, as any visitor can testify, that we have here a cowed community, broken in spirit by a powerful bureaucracy, terrified of ignoring or breaking some regulation: it is in fact far easier in spirit than Britain. It is genuinely democratic, in practice as well as in theory, and in its very atmosphere. Socially it may not be completely classless – I have yet to discover such a society – but compared to England it is like the week after a bloodless and smiling revolution.

At this time of writing, these islands have a population of just under 3,000,000. So they are not committed, as much larger industrial societies are, to over-crowding, lack of living-space, unmanageable and crime-ridden big cities, so many cars on the roads that every week end stages a gas attack. Conservation may be necessary, but the relationship between men and land and air has not disappeared. Possessing these advantages, a comparatively small population could attempt economic-social experiments, new styles of communal living, that it would take older and more densely-populated societies years and years even to plan and to discuss. So New Zealand could be important to the world just because it could be seen and accepted as the trial ground of such ideas and experiments. But only of course if it decided to ignore the old lures of wealth and power, now strangling our civilization, and if it concentrated on the heightening and deepening of the people's quality of life.

Am I pitching this too high? What about all those notorious 'dull people'? What about the farmers and their cash accounts, the businessmen and their balance sheets? What about all those massed Philistines avoiding or jeering at the arts? Well, my visit, brief though it was, made me feel that these questions are already out of date. There lingers behind them the old assumption that New Zealand is Britain's cast-off, like something sent to a jumble sale. And surely this is wrong except for a small group of elderly people, probably educated in England? All the young and most of the middle-aged know now where 'home' really is.

Almost always it is the poets, far ahead of politicians, officials, editors, who lead the way. They are, we may say, long sighted. So they stopped writing like minor English versifiers in exile. Ever since the 1930's, probably with Fairburn at the head of them, they have been New Zealanders intensely conscious of the New Zealand scene, with its seas booming, its mountains looming in their verse. But it is not simply that they have taken in the landscape, the sights and sounds of their two islands. We are considering something deeper here than regional verse. They have been increasingly aware of their personal involvement with the New Zealand national character and its possible destiny. They have been feeling strongly what a lot of other New Zealanders (who may not have read a word they have written) are at last beginning to feel. In short, being true poets they have led the way.

As I write this – and as I suggested earlier – the New Zealand arts and its culture in general need far more substantial subsidies than they are receiving at present; and not only for the cities but even more urgently for all those small towns that look alike and lack variety, sparkle, excitement. If during the next few years wise decisions are taken, then I believe the fatal exodus of promising young people would cease altogether. In its place there could be a frequent exchange of proven talent between Europe/America and New Zealand, which by then could be a small great country that would have escaped from an exhausted civilization. As it is, the *Encyclopaedia of New Zealand* offers us a list of successful expatriates, and they and their careers fill twenty-nine large pages with double columns and the tiniest print. All this says much for their parentage, upbringing, education, but even so to one well-wisher it makes melancholy reading. What a difference all those people might have made if they had stayed at home!

I realize that my references to the arts and culture may give a wrong impression of the sort of society I have in mind. I don't mean one in which a man has to sneak off to enjoy a week-end's sailing, fishing, hiking, because he ought to be attending lectures on Art History, the Development of the Symphony, the Social Significance of Later Victorian Fiction. For all I care, this man may never go near an art gallery, a concert, a poetry reading. All I suggest is that he upholds in his own way – and makes some contribution to – a community that isn't floundering in ignorance, stupidity, prejudice and bigotry. (And God knows such communities are common enough in the modern world!) He must be no longer content to live among idiotic TV-watchers. There is nothing wrong with TV as such; it can if it tries offer valuable instruction and superb entertainment; but it needs better, more discriminating viewers, just as the press in general needs more demanding intelligent readers. We can forego further mention of the arts and culture, and decide against bringing in

Education, which has too many doubtful associations, and briefly describe the community we want as follows. It must be in less danger, instead of in more and more danger, of producing robots and zombies. Its men and women must be broadening and deepening their experience, opening out and sharpening consciousness instead of closing it in and blunting it. They must be free from the sense of frustration that creates either apathy or the demand for violence. They must stop 'passing the time' and begin using and enjoying it. And because New Zealand has a small population and can be more flexible and experimental than older larger countries, because it offers more living space and real air instead of smog, I believe it has a better chance of creating such a community than any other country I know.

However, I must add this. Even if all goes wrong, if New Zealand turns into just another place with too many dull-eyed people, too much computerized technology and high-pressure advertising and salesmanship and not sufficient critical intelligence, too many pills and mental homes and too few life-enhancing values, I shall still remember with affection my visit and the people and scenes it brought me. At least in my memory New Zealand will be still a special place in a special situation.

Index